African Cookbook

An Easy African Cookbook Filled
with Authentic African Recipes

By
BookSumo Press

Published by:
http://www.booksumo.com

LEGAL NOTES

Table of Contents

Traditional Nigerian Beef Kebabs: (Suya) 7

Peanut Soup from Lagos 8

Authentic Nigerian Jollof: Traditional Chicken and Rice 9

Nigerian Coconut Cake Pops: Shuku Shuku 11

Alternative Jollof 12

Nigerian Banana Skillet 13

Benin City Fruit Salad 14

Carrot and Ginger Soup 15

Suya II: Chicken Kebabs 16

West African Kidney Beans 17

Suya II: Chicken Kebabs 18

Nigerian Lunchbox: Skewered Sirloin 19

Nigerian Vegetable Salad 20

Spicy Clove and Peanut Bowls 21

Spicy Coco Pilaf 22

Nigerian Chicken and Beef Dinner 23

Habanero and Onion Stew 24

Spicy Baked Bananas 25

Hot Sauce from Ghana 26

Nigerian Turkey Tomato Meatballs 27

How to Make Nigerian Style Plantains 28

Deep Fried Peanuts 29

House Stew: Igbo Style 30

3

West African Tilapia 31

Nigerian Vanilla Donuts 32

Banana Chicken Cutlets 33

African Kofta 34

Nigerian Fish Cakes 35

Nigerian Black Eyed Pea Casserole 36

Puff Puffs: Nigerian Sweet Fritters 37

Healthy African Tomato Salad 38

Spicy African Green Tea 39

Authentic Nigerian Grilled Lime Beef 40

Congo Inspired Tarragon Salad 41

Nigerian Banana Bread 42

Fish Kabobs Africano 43

Nigerian Citrus Sundae 44

Sweet and Zesty Chicken Stew 45

Nigerian Citrus Sundae 46

Chicken Soup with Egusi 47

West African Egg Sandwich 48

Safari Yellow Rice 49

Ghana Vanilla Ice Cream 50

Beef Bites with Orangy Lentils Casserole 51

Creamy Marinated Grilled Kabobs 53

Tipsy Mango Shanks 54

Acorn Veggies and Raisins Stew 55

Traditional Rubbed Chicken Roast 56

Cheesy Couscous Stuffed Zucchini Boats 57

Sweet Lemon and Chicken Stew 58

Chickpeas and Mussels Stew 59

Shish Veggies and Lamb Kebab 60

Cinnamon Lentils Soup 61

Harissa Seared Lamb Fillets 62

Herbed Fava Beans 63

Pecan Couscous Salad 64

Oven-Seared Spiced Beef 65

Eggs in Spicy Tomato Sauce 66

Hot Sausages & Eggs 67

Baked Veggie Omelet 68

Rice with Sausages & Potato 69

Baked Lamb & Veggie Stew 71

Almonds & Orange Pastries 72

Herbed Potato Pastries 73

Noodles with Chicken & Veggie Sauce 74

North African Breakfast Eggs 76

Spicy Roasted Chicken 77

North African Lamb with Sauce 78

Chicken and Chickpeas 79

Garbanzo Beans & Veggie Soup 80

Almond Baklawa 81

Semolina Flatbread 83

Fish & Veggie Soup 84

Spicy Eggplant 85

Spicy Lamb Sausage 86

Almond Bread with Orange Blossom Syrup 87

Spiced Flatbread 88

Semolina Pancakes 89

Dried Fruit Balls 90

Egyptian Cream Pudding 91

Egyptian Walla-Walla Salad 92

Cauliflower in Spicy Sauce 93

Egyptian Veggies Omelet 94

Peppers Filled Pastries 95

North African Vanilla Bread 96

Egyptian Cream Pudding 97

Fish Fillet Salad 98

North African Spiced Up Beans 99

West African Curry 100

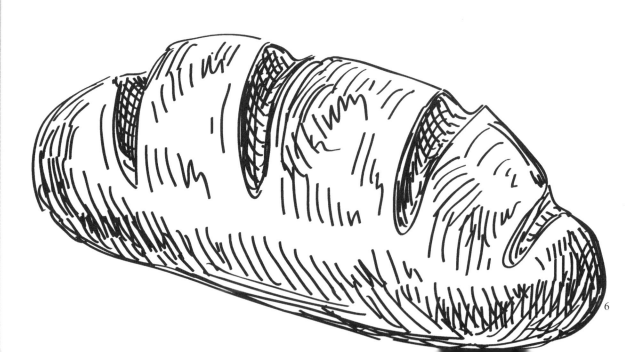

Rice
with Sausages & Potato

🍲 Prep Time: 30 mins

◉ Total Time: 1 hr 30 mins

Servings per Recipe: 4	
Calories	606.7
Fat	24.0g
Cholesterol	192.4mg
Sodium	537.8mg
Carbohydrates	73.2g
Protein	27.7g

Ingredients

4 eggs
2 zucchini
2 C. basmati rice
1 tbsp cinnamon
1/2 tbsp cumin seeds
1 tsp coriander seeds
1 tsp garlic powder
3 tbsp olive oil
1/2 lb potato
olive oil
salt and pepper
1 lb ground beef
1 onion
6 garlic cloves

3 tbsp chopped parsley
1/2 tsp coriander powder
1 tsp caraway seed
1 tsp garlic powder
1 tsp paprika
1/2 tsp cayenne pepper
1/2 tsp salt
1/2 tsp black pepper
olive oil
6 oz. tomato paste
2 C. water
4 green bell peppers, cut into thin strips
1 lemon, cut into thin semi-circles

Directions

1. Set your oven to 375 degrees F before doing anything else.
2. Set your grill to low heat and grease the grill grate.
3. In a pan of boiling water, hard boil the eggs and drain.
4. Peel the eggs and then cut into 1/4-inch strips and keep aside.
5. Cut the zucchini into 1/4-inch strips and cook on grill for about 5-10 minutes till soft.
6. In a pan, heat 3 tbsp of the oil on low heat and sauté the coriander seeds, cumin seeds, cinnamon and 1 tsp. of the garlic powder for about 8-10 minutes.
7. Stir in the rice and then add 4 C. of water.
8. Cover the pan and bring to a boil on medium heat.
9. Reduce the heat and simmer for about 20 minutes till all the liquid is absorbed.
10. Cut the potatoes in 8 wedges and place in a bowl with oil, salt and black pepper and toss to coat well.
11. Arrange the potato wedges onto a baking sheet in a single layer.

12. Cook in the oven for about 40 minutes.
13. Chop the onion and garlic very finely in a large bowl.
14. Add the beef, parsley, caraway seeds, coriander powder, cayenne, paprika and remaining 1 tsp of garlic powder and mix till well combined.
15. With your hands, make small sausages about the size of a large thumb.
16. In a large skillet, heat the oil and cook the sausages till browned completely.
17. Transfer the sausages into plate and keep aside.
18. Remove the skillet from heat and immediately, stir in the water and tomato paste.
19. Return the skillet on heat and simmer, stirring continuously for about 5 minutes.
20.   Stir in the sausages and simmer for about 30 minutes.
21. For serving, divide the rice, followed by the sausage with some sauce, zucchini, bell peppers, egg and lemon, on plates.
22. For the side dish, place the potato wedges on the plate and drizzle with the remaining pan sauce.

Traditional
Nigerian Beef Kebabs
(Suya)

🥣 Prep Time: 10 mins

◉ Total Time: 1 hr 10 mins

Servings per Recipe: 4

Calories	358
Fat	15.4
Carbohydrates	158
Protein	644
Cholesterol	5.4
Sodium	47.3

Ingredients

1 tbsp finely ground roasted peanuts
1 tsp ground cayenne pepper
1 tsp ground paprika
1 tsp salt
1/2 tsp ground ginger
1/2 tsp garlic powder
1/2 tsp onion powder

1 1/2 lb. beef tri-tip steak, cut into bite-size pieces
1 red bell pepper, cut into bite-size pieces
1/4 onion, cut into bite-size pieces
4 mushrooms, halved

Directions

1. In a bowl, add the ground peanuts, paprika, cayenne pepper, salt, ginger, onion powder and garlic powder and mix until well combined.
2. In a resealable plastic bag, add the beef and spice mixture.
3. Seal the bag and shake to coat well.
4. Refrigerate to marinate for about 30 minutes.
5. Set your outdoor grill for medium-high heat and lightly, grease the grill grate.
6. Thread the beef, bell pepper, onion, and mushrooms in alternating order onto skewers.
7. Cook on the grill for about 10-15 minutes, flipping once in the middle way.

PEANUT SOUP
from Lagos

Prep Time: 15 mins
Total Time: 45 mins

Servings per Recipe: 4
Calories	241
Fat	17.5
Carbohydrates	0g
Protein	921
Cholesterol	10.8
Sodium	13

Ingredients
4 C. chicken broth
1 jalapeño pepper, seeded and minced
1/2 C. chopped green bell pepper
1/2 C. chopped onion
1/2 C. crunchy peanut butter

Directions
1. In 1-quart pan, add the broth and chili peppers and bring to a boil.
2. Stir in the bell pepper and onion and again bring to a boil.
3. Reduce the heat to low and simmer, covered for about 10 minutes.
4. Reduce the heat to low and stir in the peanut butter.
5. Cook until peanut butter is melted, stirring continuously.

Authentic
Nigerian Jollof
(Nigerian Traditional Dinner)
(Chicken and Rice)

Prep Time: 30 mins
Total Time: 1 hr 20 mins

Servings per Recipe: 8	
Calories	703
Fat	22.8
Cholesterol	71
Sodium	942
Carbohydrates	96.3
Protein	31.7

Ingredients

Chicken:
2 lb. chicken drumsticks
1/2 large onion, diced
1 (2 inch) piece fresh ginger root, peeled and thinly sliced
2 cubes chicken bouillon, crushed
2 cloves garlic, diced
1 tbsp curry powder
1 tsp herbes de Provence
freshly ground black pepper
1 pinch cayenne pepper
1 C. water
Rice:
3 tbsp vegetable oil

1/2 large onion, diced
1 (14 oz.) can tomato sauce
1 (14 oz.) can coconut milk
1 tsp herbes de Provence
1 tsp salt
1/2 tsp ground black pepper
3 C. parboiled rice
1 (10 oz.) package frozen mixed vegetables (carrots, corn, peas)
Plantains:
4 ripe plantains, peeled and cut diagonally into 1/2-inch slices
1/2 C. canola oil for frying

Directions

1. Set your oven to 400 degrees F before doing anything else.
2. In a large Dutch oven, mix together the chicken, 1/2 onion, ginger, garlic, crushed bouillon cubes, curry powder, 1 tsp of the herbes de Provence, cayenne pepper and black pepper and cook for about 5 minutes.
3. Stir in the water and bring to a gentle boil.
4. Cook, covered for about 15 minutes.
5. Remove from the heat and with a slotted spoon, transfer the chicken into a baking dish using.
6. Through a fine-mesh sieve, strain cooking liquid.
7. Reserve 1 1/2 C. of the liquid, discarding the solids.

8. Cook the chicken in the the oven for about 30 minutes.
9. In a large pan, heat 3 tbsp of the vegetable oil over medium-low heat and cook 1/2 of the onion for about 5 minutes.
10. Stir in the tomato sauce and cook for about 5-7 minutes, stirring continuously.
11. Stir in the coconut milk, reserved chicken broth, 1 tsp of the herbes de Provence, salt and black pepper and bring to a gentle boil.
12. Stir in the rice and cook for about 15-20 minutes, stirring occasionally.
13. Stir in the frozen vegetables and cook for about 5 minutes.
14. In a large pan, heat 1/2 C. of the canola oil over medium heat and fry the plantains for about 2-3 minutes per side.
15. Transfer the plantain onto paper towels lined plate to drain.
16. Serve the jollof rice with a garnishing of the fried plantains.

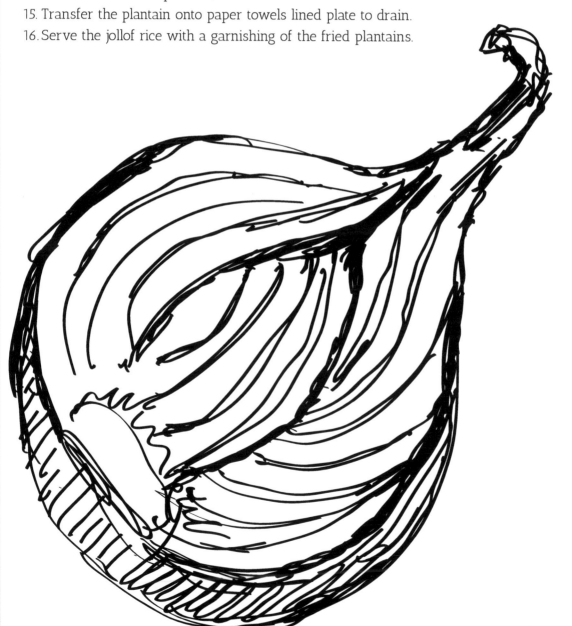

Nigerian
Coconut Cake Pops
(Shuku Shuku)

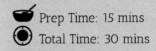 Prep Time: 15 mins

Total Time: 30 mins

Servings per Recipe: 12	
Calories	80.3
Fat	4.8g
Cholesterol	35.5mg
Sodium	60.5mg
Carbohydrates	8.4g
Protein	1.3g

Ingredients
1 C. unsweetened flaked coconut
1/4 C. caster sugar
3 egg yolks
1/2 C. self-raising flour

Directions
1. Set your oven to 350 degrees F before doing anything else.
2. In a bowl, add the sugar, coconut and egg yolks and mix until a stiff dough is formed.
3. Make about 1-inch balls from the dough and coat each ball with the flour evenly.
4. Arrange the balls onto a baking sheet about 2-inch apart.
5. Cook in the oven for about 20 minutes.

ALTERNATIVE
Jollof

Prep Time: 10 mins
Total Time: 30 mins

Servings per Recipe: 4
Calories	597.8
Fat	18.3g
Cholesterol	7.5mg
Sodium	550.6mg
Carbohydrates	96.4g
Protein	12.4g

Ingredients

2 C. rice (long grained)
1/4 C. groundnut oil
1/2 tbsp butter
1 tsp dried thyme
1/4 tsp curry powder (optional)
1 onion, sliced
1 celery, diced
1 green pepper, diced (remove the seeds & white stuff)
2 - 3 garlic cloves
1 C. chicken breast, diced not cooked preferably
1/2 inch piece ginger, peeled and grated
1 tbsp ground paprika (smoked)
2 tbsp cayenne
3 tbsp tomato paste
2 large tomatoes, chopped finely
1 carrot, cubed
1 chicken bouillon cube
1 bay leaf
2 C. chicken stock
2 C. water
1/2 C. portobello mushroom (optional)
peas
salt
1/4 C. cilantro (to garnish)

Directions

1. In a heat resistance pan, heat the oil and butter and cook the chicken breast, green pepper, onion, celery, ginger, garlic, cayenne and paprika for about 3 minutes.

2. Stir in the chopped carrots and a little salt and sauté for about 1 minute.

3. Add the tomatoes, tomato paste, thyme, curry powder and bay leaf and cook for about 3 minutes.

4. Add the frozen veggies and stir to combine.

5. Stir in the rice and sauté for about 2 minutes.

6. Add 3 C. of the stock, water, bouillon cube, salt and cook, covered for about 30 minutes.

7. Cook until the rice is soft.

8. Serve with a garnishing of the cilantro.

Nigerian
Banana Skillet

🥄 Prep Time: 10 mins
◉ Total Time: 20 mins

Servings per Recipe: 4
Calories   865.2
Fat   48.7g
Cholesterol   131.1mg
Sodium   386.7mg
Carbohydrates   111.9g
Protein   0.8g

Ingredients
1 bunch banana
16 oz. brown sugar
1 C. butter
8 oz. whipped cream

Directions
1. Peel the bananas and split down the middle and then cut in half.
2. In a skillet, melt 1 stick of the butter over medium-high heat.
3. Coat the banana slices with the melted butter.
4. Place the banana slices in the skillet and sprinkle with some brown sugar.
5. Flip and sprinkle with brown sugar.
6. Cook for about 1 minute, without stirring.
7. Flip and again sprinkle with brown sugar.
8. Repeat the procedure until all the sugar is used and banana slices are caramelized.
9. Serve hot with a topping of the whipped cream.

NOODLES
with Chicken & Veggie Sauce

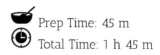
Prep Time: 45 m
Total Time: 1 h 45 m

Servings per Recipe: 8
Calories   811.6
Fat   32.8g
Cholesterol   144.7mg
Sodium   855.1mg
Carbohydrates   79.8g
Protein   46.3g

Ingredients
500 g plain flour
1/2 tsp salt
water
cornflour, to aid rolling out
1 tbsp ghee
1 1/2 kg chicken pieces
2 onions, finely chopped
1 garlic clove, minced
1 tbsp sunflower oil
1 C. of tinned chickpeas

1/4 tsp black pepper
2 1/4 tsps ras el hanout spice mix
1 liter water
1 tsp cinnamon
500 g long turnips, cut into 6ths
250 g potatoes, quartered
250 g courgettes, cut into 6ths
1 1/2 tsps salt

Directions
1. In a large bowl, sift together the flour and salt.
2. With your hands, make a well in the center.
3. Slowly, add the water, mixing till a soft dough forms.
4. Dust a smooth surface with the corn flour.
5. Divide the dough into 4 portions and roll onto the floured surface into 1-2 mm thickness.
6. With a little corn flour, dust the dough sheets and process in the pasta machine on the lowest settings.
7. Keep aside the pasta sheets for about 20-30 minutes.
8. Now, set the pasta machine to the settings that will cut the sheets into fine ribbons.
9. Again with a little corn flour, dust the pasta sheets and process in the pasta machine to have the fine ribbons.
10. Keep the noodles aside for at least 10 minutes.
11. With a little oil, gently coat the noodles and cook in the steamer for about 5 minutes.
12. Remove from steamer and drizzle with a little water to separate the noodles and steam for 5 minutes more.
13. Transfer the noodles in a large dish and mix with the ghee and a little salt.

14. For sauce in a large pan, heat the oil on medium heat and stir fry the chicken, onion, garlic and spices for about 10 minutes.
15. Stir in the vegetables, seasoning and water and cook, covered for about 40 minutes.
16. Stir in the chickpeas and cook, covered for about 20 minutes more.
17. Transfer the noodles into the serving plates and top with the chicken mixture and serve.

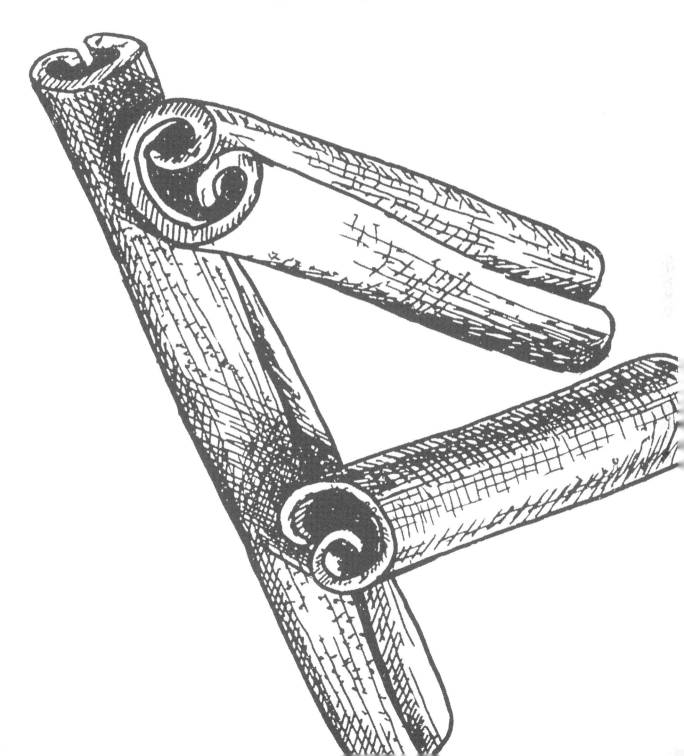

BENIN CITY
Fruit Salad

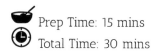 Prep Time: 15 mins

Total Time: 30 mins

Servings per Recipe: 10
Calories	136.5
Fat	1.5g
Cholesterol	0.0mg
Sodium	13.0mg
Carbohydrates	32.3g
Protein	1.5g

Ingredients
4 ripe papayas, peeled, seeded and cut into
bite-size pieces
2 red apples, cored and chopped
2 ripe bananas, peeled and sliced
1 (16 oz.) cans pineapple tidbits, well-
drained
1 C. fresh orange juice
1 tbsp granulated sugar
1/2 tsp ground cinnamon
1/3 C. sweetened flaked coconut

Directions
1. In a large bowl, add all the ingredients except the shredded coconut and toss to coat well.
2. Refrigerate, covered to chill before serving.
3. Serve with a sprinkling of the shredded coconut.

Carrot Ginger Soup

Prep Time: 20 mins
Total Time: 40 mins

Servings per Recipe: 3
Calories   381.2
Fat   26.4g
Cholesterol   0.0mg
Sodium   558.8mg
Carbohydrates   29.1g
Protein   13.1g

Ingredients

1 tbsp olive oil
1 C. chopped yellow onion
3/4 C. chopped peeled carrot
1 - 2 tsp minced peeled fresh ginger
1 dash cayenne pepper
1 C. chopped peeled sweet potato
2 1/2 C. water, divided
1/2 C. tomato juice
1/4 tsp salt

1/4 tsp black pepper
1/2 C. creamy peanut butter
5 green onions, chopped

Directions

1. In a large pan, heat the oil and cook the onions and carrots for about 3 minutes, stirring occasionally.
2. Stir in the ginger and cayenne and cook for about 1 minute.
3. Stir in the sweet potato, tomato juice, 2 C. of the water, salt and pepper and bring to a boil.
4. Reduce the heat and simmer for about 15 minutes, stirring occasionally.
5. Remove from the heat and keep aside to cool slightly.
6. In a food processor, add the soup with the peanut butter and pulse until smooth.
7. Transfer the mixture into another pan over low heat and cook until heated through. (You can add remaining 1/2 C. water to thin the soup).
8. Serve hot with a topping of the green onions.

SUYA II
(Chicken Kebabs)

Prep Time: 10 mins
Total Time: 30 mins

Servings per Recipe: 4
Calories	243.8
Fat	12.6g
Cholesterol	72.6mg
Sodium	136.4mg
Carbohydrates	6.8g
Protein	26.4g

Ingredients
1 tbsp garlic powder
1 tbsp ground ginger
1 tbsp paprika
2 tbsp cayenne powder
1 tbsp dried onion flakes
2 tbsp peanuts, finely minced
1 lb boneless skinless chicken breast
2 tbsp peanut oil

Directions
1. Set the broiler of your oven
2. In a large bowl, mix together all slices.
3. Cut the chicken into thin pieces and sprinkle with the spice mixture.
4. Keep aside for about 5 minutes.
5. Thread the chicken onto pre-soaked wooden skewers and coat with the oil.
6. Cook the skewers under broiler for about 3 minutes per side.

West African
Kidney Beans

Prep Time: 1 day
Total Time: 1 day 3 h

Servings per Recipe: 4	
Calories	247.2
Fat	15.8g
Cholesterol	0.0mg
Sodium	1399.8mg
Carbohydrates	22.7g
Protein	9.6g

Ingredients

1 1/2 C. dried kidney beans
1 small green pepper, seeded & diced
2 tsp salt
1 tsp ground cumin
2 tbsp oil
0.5 (5 1/2 oz.) cans tomato paste

1 medium onion, finely chopped
2 garlic cloves, crushed
1/4 tsp cayenne
1 tsp fresh lemon juice
1/4 C. peanut butter, smooth is best
1 C. frozen corn

Directions

1. In a large bowl of water, soak the beans overnight.
2. Drain the beans well.
3. In a large pan, add the beans and 6 C. of the water and bring to a boil.
4. Reduce the heat and simmer for about 2-2 1/2 hours, stirring occasionally.
5. In a skillet, heat the oil over medium heat and sauté the green pepper, onion and garlic until the onion is just translucent.
6. Add the cumin and stir to combine.
7. Stir in the lemon juice, tomato paste, cayenne and 1/2 C. of the water and bring to a gentle boil.
8. Reduce the heat and simmer for about 15 minutes.
9. Meanwhile, in a small bowl, add the peanut butter.
10. Slowly, add about 6 tbsp of the cooking liquid from the beans and mix well.
11. Add the peanut butter mixture into the beans and stir to combine.
12. Add the onion mixture and corn in the pan of the beans and bring to a gentle boil.
13. Reduce the heat to low and simmer, covered for about 10 minutes, stirring occasionally.
14. Serve hot.

LEMONY
Eggplant Dip

 Prep Time: 30 mins
Total Time: 45 mins

Servings per Recipe: 2
Calories   73.7
Fat   1.2g
Cholesterol   0.0mg
Sodium   588.8mg
Carbohydrates   16.2g
Protein   2.8g

Ingredients
1 eggplant, large
1 tsp sesame seeds, mashed
1/2 tsp salt
1 garlic clove, mashed
4 tbsp lemon juice
2 tbsp parsley, fresh and finely chopped

Directions
1. In a steamer, steam the eggplant for about 25 minutes.
2. Carefully, scrape out the soft flesh from the skin and transfer into a bowl.
3. Add the sesame paste, garlic, lemon juice and salt and stir to combine.
4. Serve with a sprinkling of the parsley.

Nigerian Lunchbox
Skewered Sirloin

🍳 Prep Time: 10 m
◉ Total Time: 30 m

Servings per Recipe: 4
Calories	299.5
Fat	21.7g
Cholesterol	79.5mg
Sodium	400.0mg
Carbohydrates	3.6g
Protein	23.8g

Ingredients

1 lb. lean beef, boneless (sirloin)
1 1/2 tbsp natural-style peanut butter (ground roasted peanuts)
1 1/2 tbsp vegetable oil
1 tbsp ginger powder
1/2 tbsp red cayenne pepper

1/2 tsp ground cloves
2 bouillon cubes

Directions

1. Cut the meat into 1/2-inch thick slices.
2. In a small bowl, mix together the ground peanut, ginger, pepper, cloves and bouillon.
3. Coat the meat with spice mixture and then, brush with oil.
4. Thread meat onto 4 large wide skewers.
5. Cook the skewers onto grill until desired doneness.

NIGERIAN
Vegetable Salad

Prep Time: 15 mins
Total Time: 30 mins

Servings per Recipe: 8	
Calories	181.7
Fat	9.9 g
Cholesterol	1.9 mg
Sodium	148.2 mg
Carbohydrates	21.4 g
Protein	4.9 g

Ingredients

SALAD
1 C. Yukon gold potato, 3/4-inch peeled, cooked till tender
1 C. sweet potato, 3/4-inch, peeled, cooked till tender
1 C. cauliflower, lightly cooked florets
1 C. broccoli, lightly cooked florets
4 carrots, peeled and sliced into ribbons
3 small canned beets (1/4-inch slices)
10 bibb lettuce
10 leaves red cabbage
VINAIGRETTE DRESSING
1 tbsp fresh thyme, chopped
2 tbsp fresh lemon juice
2 tbsp red wine vinegar
1 tbsp Dijon mustard
1/4 tsp sugar
1/8 tsp fresh ground black pepper
1/4 C. extra virgin olive oil
2 ground dried chile
1/2 C. prepared seafood cocktail sauce
1/4 C. mayonnaise
salt
1/4 tsp fresh ground black pepper

Directions

1. For the vinaigrette: in a bowl, add the thyme, oil, lemon juice, vinegar, Dijon mustard, sugar and 1/8 tsp of the black pepper and beat until well combined.

2. For the salad: in a large bowl, mix together the potatoes, cauliflower, broccoli and carrots.

3. Add the dressing and gently, toss to coat well.

4. Arrange lettuce and cabbage leaves alternately onto a large chilled platter and top with the potato mixture, followed by the beets.

5. Serve the vegetables as a salad.

Spicy Clove
and Peanut Bowls

Prep Time: 10 m
Total Time: 30 m

Servings per Recipe: 4
Calories	362.7
Fat	24.2g
Cholesterol	46.4mg
Sodium	223.7mg
Carbohydrates	15.6g
Protein	24.0g

Ingredients

1 tsp canola oil
1 onion, finely chopped
1 - 2 garlic clove, minced
1 1/2 tbsp fresh ginger, grated
1 jalapeño pepper, diced
2 chicken breasts, finely chopped
2 - 3 medium tomatoes, chopped
1 carrot, peeled and grated
1/2 - 1 tsp turmeric

1 tsp berbere, spice powder
1/2 tsp ground cloves
black pepper, to taste
1 - 2 tsp sugar
3 - 4 C. water
1/2 - 1 C. crunchy peanut butter
peanuts, for garnish (optional)
1 dash lemons (optional)

Directions

1. In a medium pan, heat the oil over medium heat and cook the onions, ginger and garlic until the onion is translucent.
2. Add the jalapeño and cook for several minutes.
3. Add the chicken, turmeric, berbere and cloves and cook until the chicken is cooked through.
4. Stir in the carrots and tomatoes and cook for about 5 minutes, stirring occasionally.
5. Add the water and bring to a boil.
6. Add the peanut butter and stir to combine.
7. Reduce the heat to medium - low and simmer for about 5-10 minutes, stirring continuous.
8. Serve hot.

SPICY
Coco Pilaf

🍜 Prep Time: 20 mins
🕐 Total Time: 40 mins

Servings per Recipe: 4

Calories	759.3
Fat	32.6g
Cholesterol	0.0mg
Sodium	637.5mg
Carbohydrates	112.5g
Protein	7.5g

Ingredients
1 C. rice
1 (15 oz.) cans coconut milk
1 (29 oz.) cans diced tomatoes
4 medium habanero peppers
1 small green pepper (diced)
1 small yellow onion (diced)
1/4 C. vegetable oil
1 tsp sea salt
1 tsp black pepper

Directions
1. In the pan of the water, cook the rice for about 10 - 15 minutes.
2. In the pan, heat the vegetable oil and sauté the onions with black pepper for about 1 minute.
3. Stir in the diced tomatoes, habaneros, coconut milk and salt and cook, covered for about 7 minutes.
4. Stir in the rice and cook, covered for about 7 minutes.
5. Add the green peppers and simmer until all the liquid is absorbed.

Nigerian
Chicken and Beef Dinner

🍳 Prep Time: 20 m
◉ Total Time: 1h 30 m

Servings per Recipe: 8
Calories   667.5
Fat   46.0g
Cholesterol   178.5mg
Sodium   623.0mg
Carbohydrates   14.3g
Protein   52.0g

Ingredients
1 1/2 lb. chicken thighs
1 1/2 lb. chicken legs
2 tbsp vegetable oil
1 lb. beef stew meat, cubed
2 medium onions, chopped
1 green bell pepper, chopped
1 (28 oz.) cans tomatoes, chopped
1 tsp salt
2 tbsp ground red pepper

1 C. peanut butter (smooth kind)
cooked mashed sweet potatoes
cooked rice

Directions
1. In a large Dutch oven, heat the oil and cook the chicken for about 15 minutes.
2. Transfer the chicken into a bowl, reserving the drippings in the pan.
3. In the same pan, add the beef, onion and green pepper and cook until beef is browned completely.
4. Drain the grease from the pan.
5. Stir in undrained tomatoes, salt and red pepper and bring to a boil.
6. Reduce the heat and simmer, covered for about 30 minutes.
7. Stir in the cooked chicken and simmer for about 20 minutes.
8. In a small pan, melt the peanut butter over low heat.
9. Add the melted peanut butter into the chicken mixture and again, bring to a boil.
10. Reduce the heat and simmer, covered for about 20 minutes, skimming the fat occasionally.
11. Serve hot with mashed sweet potatoes or hot cooked rice.

HABANERO
Onion Stew

🍲 Prep Time: 20 mins
🕐 Total Time: 25 mins

Servings per Recipe: 2
Calories	1054.9
Fat	108.9g
Cholesterol	0.0mg
Sodium	1184.2mg
Carbohydrates	22.2g
Protein	4.3g

Ingredients
1 bulb onion, chopped
2 C. beans, rinsed
3 tomatoes
5 habanero peppers
1/2 C. peanut oil
1 tsp seasoning
1 tsp salt
1/2 C. palm oil

Directions
1. In a pan of the boiling water, cook the beans and half of the onions, covered and until beans become soft.
2. Sprinkle with a little salt and cook until all the water is absorbed.
3. Meanwhile, in a food processor, add the remaining onion, tomatoes and pepper and pulse until pureed.
4. In another small pan, heat the palm oil.
5. Add the groundnut oil and heat until well combined.
6. Add the pureed mixture, seasoning and salt and stir fry for a few minutes.
7. Serve the pureed mixture with the stew.

African
Chicken and Okra

🥣 Prep Time: 30 m

◉ Total Time: 1h 30 m

Servings per Recipe: 6

Calories	621.2
Fat	41.3g
Cholesterol	103.5mg
Sodium	988.7mg
Carbohydrates	29.2g
Protein	35.6g

Ingredients

3 - 3 1/2 lb. chicken pieces (10 pieces)
1 tsp salt
1 (15 oz.) cans whole tomatoes with juice
1/4 C. water
2 tbsp tomato paste
1/4 C. peanut oil
1 medium onion, chopped
4 garlic cloves, minced and mashed to a
paste with 1 tsp salt
1 1/4 tsp cayenne
1/2 C. smooth peanut butter, at room temperature
1 3/4 C. chicken broth
1 lb sweet potato
1 (10 oz.) frozen okra, thawed
cooked rice

Directions

1. Place the chicken onto a baking sheet in a single layer and sprinkle with the salt.
2. Keep aside at room temperature for about 30 minutes.
3. In a food processor, add the tomatoes with their juice and pulse until finely chopped.
4. Transfer the tomato paste in a small bowl with the water and mix until smooth.
5. With the paper towels, pat dry the chicken.
6. In a 10-12-inch heavy skillet, heat the oil over medium-high heat and cook the chicken in 3-4 batches for about 6 minutes, stirring occasionally.
7. Transfer the chicken into a 6-7-quart heavy pot, leaving about 2 tbsp of the fat into skillet.
8. In the same skillet, add onion over medium heat and cook for about 2-3 minutes, stirring occasionally.
9. Add the onion mixture in the pan of the chicken with the tomatoes, tomato paste mixture, garlic paste, and cayenne and stir to combine.
10. In a bowl, add the peanut butter and 1 C. of the broth and beat until smooth.
11. In the pan of the chicken, stir in the peanut butter mixture with the remaining 3/4 C. of broth and bring to a boil.
12. Reduce the heat and simmer, covered for about 25-30 minutes, stirring occasionally.
13. Peel the sweet potato and cut into 1-inch chunks.
14. In the pan of the chicken, stir in the sweet potato and okra and simmer, covered for about 10-12 minutes.

HOT SAUCE
from Ghana

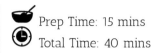 Prep Time: 15 mins
Total Time: 40 mins

Servings per Recipe: 1
Calories   1268.4
Fat   131.3g
Cholesterol   0.0mg
Sodium   18.2mg
Carbohydrates   26.7g
Protein   5.2g

Ingredients
60 g piri-piri chilies, dried
150 g scotch bonnet chilies
150 ml vegetable oil
50 g habanero chilies
100G DRIED ANCHOVIES
anchovy fillet
1/2 tsp sugar
salt and black pepper

Directions
1. Soak the dried chilies overnight.
2. Drain the chilies well.
3. With a pestle and mortar, pound the chillies into a paste.
4. Add the anchovies and pound to a paste.
5. Add the remaining chilies and pound to a paste.
6. In a heavy-bottomed pan, heat the oil over high heat and sir fry the chili paste, sugar, salt and black pepper until all the liquid is absorbed.
7. Transfer the sauce into an airtight jar along with all the oil.
8. Seal the jar and keep aside to cool.
9. Preserve in refrigerator.

NIGERIAN
Turkey Tomato Meatballs

🥣 Prep Time: 20 mins
🕐 Total Time: 40 mins

Servings per Recipe: 4

Calories	568.5
Fat	28.2g
Cholesterol	156.6mg
Sodium	630.4mg
Carbohydrates	32.8g
Protein	49.7g

Ingredients

2 lb. ground turkey
1 medium sweet potato, peeled and grated
2 medium carrots, peeled and grated
1 large onion, peeled and grated
1 tsp pepper
hot pepper sauce
salt
3 tbsp palm oil
2 medium onions, finely chopped

1 (8 oz.) cans tomato paste
3 tomatoes, chopped and mashed
1 bay leaf
nutmeg (to taste)
salt
black pepper
cayenne pepper (to taste)

Directions

1. For the meatballs: in a bowl, add the turkey, sweet potato, carrots, onion, hot pepper sauce, salt and 1 tsp of the pepper and mix until well combined.

2. Freeze the balls for at least 10 minutes.

3. For the sauce: in a frying pan, heat 3 tbsp of the palm oil and sauté the onions for a few minutes.

4. Stir in the onions, 3 tomatoes, tomato paste, bay leaf, nutmeg, salt, black pepper, cayenne pepper and enough water and bring to a gentle boil.

5. Reduce the heat and simmer for about 10 minutes.

6. Meanwhile, in another greased frying pan, cook the meatballs until browned completely.

7. Add enough tomato sauce to cover the meatballs with a few splashes of hot pepper sauce and bring to a boil.

8. Reduce the heat o low and cook, covered for about 20 minutes.

9. Serve hot.

HOW TO MAKE
Nigerian Style Plantains

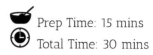 Prep Time: 15 mins
Total Time: 30 mins

Servings per Recipe: 4
Calories	308.5
Fat	10.8g
Cholesterol	0.0mg
Sodium	7.1mg
Carbohydrates	57.0g
Protein	2.3g

Ingredients
4 ripe plantains, cut in half crosswise and
lengthwise peeled
3 tbsp oil

Directions
1. In a skillet, heat about 1/2-inch oil over medium heat and sauté the plantains in batches until lightly browned from both sides.
2. Transfer the plantains onto a paper towel-lined plate to drain.

Deep
Fried Peanuts

Prep Time: 10 m
Total Time: 30 m

Servings per Recipe: 4
Calories	782.7
Fat	69.8g
Cholesterol	0.0mg
Sodium	921.9mg
Carbohydrates	24.3g
Protein	26.8g

Ingredients
1 lb. roasted peanuts
1/4 C. peanut oil
peanut oil, for frying

Directions
1. In a food processor, add nuts and pulse until finely ground.
2. Add enough oil and pulse until a smooth paste is formed.
3. With wet hands, squeeze the paste to remove the excess oil.
4. Make balls from the peanut paste.
5. In a deep skillet, heat the frying oil to 350 - 375 degrees F and fry the balls for about 3 - 4 minutes.
6. Can be served hot or cold.

HOUSE STEW
(Igbo Style)

Prep Time: 15 mins
Total Time: 30 mins

Servings per Recipe: 10
Calories	609.5
Fat	46.0g
Cholesterol	138.5mg
Sodium	1789.3mg
Carbohydrates	12.0g
Protein	36.9g

Ingredients

6 chicken thighs, on bone
3 lb. stewing beef
5 - 6 medium hot house tomatoes
2 (6 oz.) cans tomato paste
1/2 red pepper
1 - 2 jalapeño
1 red onion
1 white onion
5 garlic cloves

3 tbsp hot sauce (optional)
2 tbsp salt
1/2 C. vegetable oil
fresh ground black pepper
fresh basil
fresh cilantro
fresh spinach
fresh thyme

Directions

1. In a large pan, add the meat, onions, vegetable oil, salt and enough water to cover and bring to a boil.

2. Cook until meat is tender.

3. Meanwhile, in a food processor, add together tomatoes, garlic, tomatoes paste, jalapeño, red pepper and fresh herbs and pulse until pureed.

4. Drain the liquid, leaving about 1 1/2 C. of the cup in side.

5. In the pan of stew, add the puree mixture and cook, covered for about 1 hour.

6. In the last 15 minutes of cooking stir in the spinach.

7. Serve hot.

West African
Tilapia

Prep Time: 1 h
Total Time: 1 h 30 m

Servings per Recipe: 2	
Calories	458.7
Fat	7.7g
Cholesterol	227.0mg
Sodium	5736.0mg
Carbohydrates	2.2g
Protein	95.0g

Ingredients
1/4 C. soy sauce
2 tbsp very hot dried red peppers
1 tbsp salt
2 lb. tilapia fillets

Directions
1. Keep the fish at room temperature for about 1 hour before cooking.
2. In a bowl, add the soy sauce, salt and pepper and mix until smooth.
3. Coat the whole fish with the soy sauce mixture generously.
4. Set your oven to 400 degrees F before doing anything else.
5. With a piece of the foil, wrap the fish and cook in the oven for about 2 hours.

NIGERIAN
Vanilla Donuts

Prep Time: 30 mins
Total Time: 1 h 30 mins

Servings per Recipe: 3
Calories	6485.5
Fat	585.4g
Cholesterol	0.0mg
Sodium	2352.1mg
Carbohydrates	291.8g
Protein	34.4g

Ingredients
4 C. warm water
2 1/4 oz. active dry yeast
6 C. bread flour
2 tbsp sugar
1 1/4 C. sugar
1 tbsp salt
1 tbsp vanilla extract
1/2 gallon canola oil

Directions
1. In a bowl, dissolve 2 tbsp of the sugar and yeast into the water.
2. Keep aside for about 7 minutes.
3. Transfer the mixture into a large bowl.
4. Add the remaining sugar, salt, and vanilla extract and mix well until dissolved.
5. Sift 6 C. of the flour into the yeast mixture and mix well.
6. Now, with your hand mix until all the bumps are smooth.
7. With a plastic wrap, cover the dough and and keep at a warm place for about 1 1/2 hours.
8. Make small balls from the dough.
9. In a pan, heat about 2-inch of the oil over medium heat for about 15 minutes.
10. Reduce the heat for about 3 minutes.
11. Add the balls and increase the heat.
12. Fry the balls for about 3-4 minutes

Banana
Chicken Cutlets

Prep Time: 10 m
Total Time: 40 m

Servings per Recipe: 6
Calories   675.6
Fat   50.1g
Cholesterol   92.8mg
Sodium   92.5mg
Carbohydrates   26.9g
Protein   31.5g

Ingredients
6 chicken breasts
6 bananas
1 C. canola oil

Directions
1. Set your oven to 350 degrees F before doing anything else.
2. Wash the chicken breasts and coat with into the oil.
3. Peel the bananas and then, mash them.
4. Arrange chicken onto a baking sheet and cover each piece with mashed banana.
5. Cook in the oven for about 30 minutes.

Banana Chicken Cutlets

37

AFRICAN
Kofta

Prep Time: 20 mins
Total Time: 40 mins

Servings per Recipe: 4
Calories   252.6
Fat   13.9g
Cholesterol   127.7mg
Sodium   101.8mg
Carbohydrates   3.1g
Protein   26.9g

Ingredients
500 g lean ground beef
1 tsp ground dried chile
1 onion, finely chopped
1 egg, beaten
2 tbsp fresh coriander, chopped
1 tsp nutmeg, ground
salt
oil, for brushing

Directions
1. In a large bowl, add all the ingredients except oil and mix until well combined.
2. Refrigerate, covered for about 1 hour.
3. Preheat the barbecue grill.
4. Divide the beef mixture into 12 equal sized portions.
5. Shaped each portion into 2-inch long sausage and squeeze each firmly.
6. Carefully, push 4 greased skewers through sausage, moulding them firmly on the skewer.
7. Coat the kebab with oil evenly and place on the grill over the hot coal.
8. Cook for about 7-10 minutes, flipping frequently.
9. Serve hot.

Nigerian
Fish Cakes

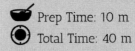 Prep Time: 10 m

Total Time: 40 m

Servings per Recipe: 8

Calories	257.2
Fat	18.1g
Cholesterol	259.0mg
Sodium	2336.5mg
Carbohydrates	4.9g
Protein	18.1g

Ingredients

1 lb. pea beans, soaked in water to cover overnight (any white beans will do)
1 tbsp salt
1/2 lb. fresh tomato, cut in 1/4 inch cubes
1/2 lb. yellow onion, finely chopped
1 lb. cooked shrimp, in 1/2 inch pieces
1 tbsp salt
1/4 tsp black pepper
1/4 tsp cayenne pepper
6 large eggs, beaten lightly
1/2 C. peanut oil

Directions

1. Drain the water from soaked beans.
2. In a 1 quart pan, add the beans, 1 tbsp of salt and enough water to cover and bring to a boil.
3. Reduce the heat and simmer until tender.
4. Through a sieve, drain the beans and transfer into a 3 quart bowl.
5. Add the shrimp, eggs, tomatoes, onions, cayenne pepper, 1 tbsp of salt and black pepper and mix well.
6. In a large skillet, heat the peanut oil.
7. With a heaping tbsp, drop the mixture and cook until golden brown from both sides.

NIGERIAN
Black Eyed Pea Casserole

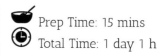

Prep Time: 15 mins
Total Time: 1 day 1 h

Servings per Recipe: 12
Calories	219.6
Fat	10.9g
Cholesterol	75.4mg
Sodium	154.3mg
Carbohydrates	19.1g
Protein	12.0g

Ingredients
PUREE
2 C. dried black-eyed peas, soaked overnight and skinned
1 onion, coarsely chopped
1 tbsp tomato paste
1 tsp ground red pepper
1/2 tsp salt
1/2 C. peanut oil
1 tbsp maggi seasoning, sauce

1 tsp curry powder
LAYERS
1 small onion, chopped
1/2 green bell pepper, chopped
3 hardboiled egg, peeled and sliced
1/2 lb. shrimp, cooked and peeled
1 C. cooked meat, diced

Directions
1. In a large bowl of water, soak the black-eyed peas overnight.
2. Drain the peas and remove skins by rubbing the peas together in water.
3. Drain again and discard the skins.
4. Set your oven to 375 degrees F and grease a 9-inch loaf pan.
5. In a food processor, add the soaked skinned black eyed peas, onion, tomato paste, red pepper and salt and pulse until smooth. (You can, add 4-6 tbsp of water).
6. Transfer the mixture into a bowl and stir in the oil, Maggi sauce and curry powder.
7. In a small bowl, mix together the chopped onions and green peppers.
8. Pour 1 1/2 C. of the pea puree into the prepared pan and top with half of the shrimp, half of the onion mixture, 1 C. of the pea puree, egg slices, chopped meat, 1 more C. of puree over meat, remaining shrimp, remaining onion mixture and peas puree.
9. With a piece of foil, cover the pan and cook in the oven for about 1 hour.
10. Remove the foil and cook for about 15 minutes.
11. Remove from the oven and keep aside to cool in pan for about 20 minutes before turning out onto rack.

Puff Puffs
(Nigerian Sweet Fritters)

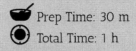 Prep Time: 30 m

Total Time: 1 h

Servings per Recipe: 10	
Calories	1985.8
Fat	186.8g
Cholesterol	83.2mg
Sodium	830.0mg
Carbohydrates	74.5g
Protein	8.4g

Ingredients
5 C. all-purpose flour
3 large eggs
9 tbsp margarine
1/4 C. water
1 tbsp salt
1/2 tsp baking powder

1/4 tsp nutmeg
1 1/3 C. sugar
1/2 gallon canola oil (for frying, the best)

Directions
1. In a large bowl, sift together the flour, baking powder, nutmeg and salt.
2. Add the sugar and mix well.
3. Add the butter to the flour and mix until well combined.
4. In another bowl, add the eggs and water and beat well.
5. Add the egg mixture into the flour mixture and with your hands, knead the mixture for about 1 minute.
6. Refrigerate the dough for about 30 minutes.
7. Shape the dough into a ball and then cut into 4 equal sized portions.
8. Place each dough portion onto a floured surface and roll thinly.
9. Now, cut into 1/6-inch thickness with 1/2-inch width strips. This should
10. Then, cut each strip into squares.
11. In a large skillet, heat the oil over medium-high heat for about 20 minutes.
12. Reduce the heat to low for about 5 minutes and fry the chin chin in batches for about 3-4 minutes.

HEALTHY
African Tomato Salad

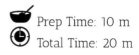
Prep Time: 10 m
Total Time: 20 m

Servings per Recipe: 1
Calories	37.8
Fat	0.4g
Cholesterol	0.0mg
Sodium	81.3mg
Carbohydrates	7.8g
Protein	3.3g

Ingredients
100 g Baby Spinach
20 g groundnuts
40 g tomatoes
2 tbsp lemon juice

Directions
1. Wash the spinach and drain well.
2. In a large bowl, place the spinach and groundnuts and toss to coat well.
3. Drizzle with the lemon juice and serve with a decoration of the tomato slices.

Spicy
African Green Tea

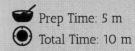 Prep Time: 5 m

Total Time: 10 m

Servings per Recipe: 1
Calories   0.0
Fat   0.0g
Cholesterol   0.0mg
Sodium   8.8mg
Carbohydrates   0.0g
Protein   0.0g

Ingredients
2 tsp green tea
2 1/2 C. simmering water
6 -9 fresh sage leaves
sugar, to taste

Directions
1. In a pitcher add all the ingredients and steep for about 4 - 5 minutes.
2. Serve warm in small glass tea cups.

AUTHENTIC
Nigerian Grilled Lime Beef

Prep Time: 2 h
Total Time: 2 h 30 m

Servings per Recipe: 5
Calories   361.0
Fat   26.9g
Cholesterol   55.3mg
Sodium   282.4mg
Carbohydrates   5.5g
Protein   26.0g

Ingredients

1 lb. top round beef (wide and long as possible cut of meat)
wooden skewer, soaked 1 hour (or bamboo skewers)
MARINADE
1/2 C. natural-style peanut butter, smooth and unsweetened
1/2 tsp ground red pepper (to taste)
1/2 tsp salt

1/2 tsp ground ginger
2 tbsp peanut oil
1 tbsp lime juice

Directions

1. For the marinade: in a bowl, add all the ingredients and mix until a smooth paste is formed.
2. Coat each meat strip with marinade generously and arrange into a glass pan.
3. Refrigerate, covered for at least 2 hours.
4. Soak wooden or bamboo skewers in cold water for at least 1 hour before using.
5. Set the broiler of your oven.
6. Thread meat onto pre-soaked skewers.
7. Cook the skewers under broiler for about 15-20 minutes, flipping once in the middle way.

Congo
Tarragon Salad

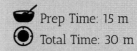 Prep Time: 15 m

Total Time: 30 m

Servings per Recipe: 4
Calories   911.6
Fat   88.5g
Cholesterol   94.4mg
Sodium   52.1mg
Carbohydrates   30.0g
Protein   5.7g

Ingredients
DRESSING
4 tbsp sugar
2 tsp sugar
1 dash Tabasco sauce
1/2 tsp Dijon-style mustard
1 tsp dried tarragon
2 egg yolks
1 dash black pepper
SALAD
2/3 C. tarragon vinegar

3/4 C. canola oil
3/4 C. olive oil
1 head romaine lettuce, washed and dried
2 green onions, sliced
1/4 C. almonds, slivered or flaked, toasted
1 (11 oz.) cans mandarin oranges in juice, drained

Directions
1. For the dressing: in food processor, add the sugar, egg yolks, mustard, tarragon, Tabasco and pepper, and mustard and pulse until welll combined.
2. While the motor is running, slowly add the vinegar.
3. While the motor is running, slowly add the oils in a thin stream and pulse until well combined.
4. Transfer the dressing into a bowl and refrigerate until using.
5. For the salad: tear the cleaned romaine into bite sized pieces.
6. In a large salad bowl, add the romaine, sliced green onions, half of the orange and desired amount of the dressing and toss to coat well.
7. Serve with a topping of the remaining oranges and almonds.

NIGERIAN
Banana Bread

Prep Time: 20 m
Total Time: 1 h 30 m

Servings per Recipe: 8
Calories   562.4
Fat   29.4g
Cholesterol   77.0mg
Sodium   313.8mg
Carbohydrates   65.6g
Protein   13.4g

Ingredients
1/2 C. butter, softened
1 C. sugar
2 eggs, well beaten
3 bananas, mashed
1 C. of your favorite peanut butter
1 tsp baking powder
2 C. wheat flour
2 tsp vanilla extract
1 C. chopped pecans (optional)

Directions
1. Set your oven to 325 degrees F before doing anything else and grease and flour a large loaf pan.
2. In a bowl, add the butter and sugar and beat until creamy.
3. Add the bananas, eggs and peanut butter and mix until well combined.
4. Add the remaining ingredients in the order listed and mix until a thick and sticky dough is formed.
5. Place the mixture into the prepared pan evenly.
6. Cook in the oven for about 1 hour.

Fish
Kabobs Africano

🥘 Prep Time: 2 h
◉ Total Time: 2 h 30 m

Servings per Recipe: 4
Calories   451.0
Fat   25.5g
Cholesterol   149.8mg
Sodium   190.6mg
Carbohydrates   7.8g
Protein   45.9g

Ingredients

2 lb. swordfish steaks, cut into large cubes
3 tbsp olive oil
1/2 lemon, juice of
1 garlic clove, crushed
1 tsp paprika
3 tomatoes, quartered
2 small onions, cut into wedges

salt & freshly ground black pepper

Directions

1. In a large dish, place the fish cubes.
2. In a owl, mix together the lemon juice, oil, garlic, paprika and seasonings.
3. Place the oil mixture over the fish evenly.
4. With clear film, cover the baking dish loosely and refrigerate to marinate for up to 2 hours.
5. Thread the fish cubes onto skewers, alternating with the tomato and onion.
6. Cook the kebabs onto grill for about 7-10 minutes, coating with the remaining marinade and flipping occasionally.

NIGERIAN
Citrus Sundae

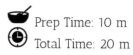

Prep Time: 10 m
Total Time: 20 m

Servings per Recipe: 4
Calories	167.1
Fat	4.3g
Cholesterol	15.8mg
Sodium	30.6mg
Carbohydrates	32.9g
Protein	2.3g

Ingredients
1 mango, fresh
2 bananas
2 tbsp lemon juice
4 tbsp orange juice
4 scoops vanilla ice cream

Directions
1. Peel the mango and then, chop finely.
2. Peel the bananas ant cut into rounds finely.
3. In a large bowl, add the fruit, lemon and orange juice and gently, toss to coat.
4. Place one scoop of ice cream in a sundae dish and top with 1/4 of the mixed fruit.
5. Repeat with the remaining ice cream and fruit.

Sweet and Zesty Chicken Stew

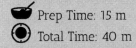 Prep Time: 15 m
Total Time: 40 m

Servings per Recipe: 8
Calories	312.3
Fat	7.2g
Cholesterol	76.8mg
Sodium	206.1mg
Carbohydrates	30.7g
Protein	30.5g

Ingredients

1/4 C. fresh lemon juice
2 tbsp honey
2 garlic cloves, crushed
1 tsp ground turmeric
1 tsp ground cumin
1 tsp ground cinnamon
1/4 tsp cayenne pepper
8 large skinless chicken breasts
8 wedges preserved lemons

1 1/2 C. chicken stock
1/3 C. slivered almonds
2 tsp olive oil
1 small yellow onion, halved, finely chopped
1 small red Chile, deseeded, finely chopped
1 C. couscous
1/3 C. currants
1/3 C. fresh coriander leaves, firmly packed

Directions

1. Get a casserole dish: mix in it the lemon juice, honey, garlic. Turmeric, cumin, cinnamon and cayenne pepper.
2. Place the chicken in the casserole and coat it with the mix. Cover it with a plastic wrap and place it in the fridge for 3 to 8 h.
3. Before you do anything preheat the oven to 360 F.
4. Drain the chicken from the marinade and reserve it. Place the chicken in a roasting pan and place the preserved lemon on it.
5. Place it in the oven to cook for 22 min.
6. Pour 1/2 C. of stock with the reserved marinade in a large pan. Cook them until they start boiling. Keeps it boiling for 6 min until it thickens?
7. Place a small skillet over medium heat. Toast in it the almonds for 3 min. place them aside.
8. Heat the oil in the same pan then cook in it the onion with chili for 3 min.
9. Stir in the rest of the stock then cook them until they start boiling.
10. Turn off the heat and combine in the couscous. Put on the lid and let it sit for 6 min.
11. Fluff the couscous with a fork then pour the thick marinade on it. Stir in the almonds and currants. Cook them for 3 min over low heat.
12. Turn off the heat then serve your couscous warm with the roasted chicken.
13. Enjoy.

THE SIMPLEST
African Chicken & Rice

🥣 Prep Time: 30 m
🕐 Total Time: 1 h 30 m

Servings per Recipe: 6
Calories	670.7
Fat	39.3g
Cholesterol	170.2mg
Sodium	611.1mg
Carbohydrates	30.0g
Protein	46.2g

Ingredients
3 lb. broiler-fryer chickens, cut up
2 tbsp peanut oil
1 medium onion, chopped
1 (16 oz.) cans canned tomatoes, cut up
1 1/4 C. chicken broth
1 bay leaf
1/2 tsp ground ginger
1/2 tsp cinnamon
1/2 tsp dried thyme, crushed

1/2 tsp salt
1/4 tsp ground red pepper
1 C. long grain rice
1 tbsp parsley, snipped

Directions
1. In large skillet, heat the oil and cook the chicken pieces for about 15 minutes.
2. Transfer the chicken into a plate and keep aside, reserving drippings in the pan.
3. Add onion to drippings and cook until tender.
4. Stir in the chicken, undrained tomatoes, broth, thyme, bay leaf, ginger, cinnamon, salt and ground red pepper and bring to a boil.
5. Reduce the heat and simmer, covered for about 30 minutes, skimming the fat occasionally.
6. Stir in the rice and simmer, covered for about 30 minutes.
7. Discard the bay leaf and serve with a sprinkling of the parsley.

Chicken
Soup with Egusi

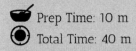
Prep Time: 10 m
Total Time: 40 m

Servings per Recipe: 4
Calories	1121.1
Fat	80.5g
Cholesterol	337.6mg112
Sodium	1276.0mg
Carbohydrates	14.0g
Protein	82.6g

Ingredients
EGUSI PASTE
1 C. egusi seeds
1/2 large Spanish onion, chopped
10 medium raw shrimp, deveined and peeled
1/4 C. water
STEW
1/4 C. canola oil
1/2 large Spanish onion, finely chopped
1/2 green bell pepper, chopped

5 oz. frozen chopped spinach, thawed and keep liquid
2 (5 1/2 oz.) cans tomato paste
1 tsp cayenne pepper
3 1/4 C. beef broth
2 whole chickens, cooked from the deli department (2 lb. each)

Directions
1. For the egusi paste: in a blender, add the egusi seeds and pulse until chopped.
2. Add the onion and shrimp and pulse until a smooth paste is formed.
3. For the stew: in a large pan, heat the oil and cook the onion until translucent.
4. Stir in the green pepper, spinach with moisture from package, tomato paste,spice and broth and simmer, covered for about 20 minutes, stirring occasionally.
5. Meanwhile, remove the skin from roaster chickens and with your hands, tear off chunks of the meat.
6. Add the chicken meat into the stew and bring to a gentle boil.
7. Stir in the paste and simmer for about 10 minutes, stirring occasionally.

WEST AFRICAN
Egg Sandwich

 Prep Time: 15 m

Total Time: 30 m

Servings per Recipe: 2
Calories	1699.0
Fat	23.7g
Cholesterol	558.0mg
Sodium	2851.9mg
Carbohydrates	290.9g
Protein	79.5g

Ingredients
1 baguette
6 eggs
1 C. very loosely packed Baby Spinach,
chopped (about a handful)
1 tbsp chopped green onion
1/8 tsp paprika, or for heat, cayenne
salt
pepper
butter or oil, for cooking

Directions
1. In a bowl, add the eggs, baby spinach, green onion, paprika, salt and pepper and beat until well combined.
2. Split the baguette and cut into desired sized sandwich lengths.
3. Arrange the bread slices onto a broiler pa and cook under the broiler until toasted and golden brown.
4. Meanwhile, cook the eggs until scrambled.
5. Place the scrambled eggs inside the bread and with parchment paper, wrap them.

Safari
Yellow Rice

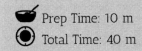 Prep Time: 10 m

Total Time: 40 m

Servings per Recipe: 4

Calories	639.9
Fat	28.6g
Cholesterol	1.8mg
Sodium	146.0mg
Carbohydrates	86.1g
Protein	12.1g

Ingredients
1 white onion, chopped
1 chili pepper, finely chopped
1 (14 oz.) cans coconut milk
2 tbsp sunflower oil
1 C. chicken stock
salt

1/2 tsp turmeric
1/2 tsp thyme
2 C. basmati rice

Directions
1. In a large pan, heat the oil over medium heat and cook the onions and chili pepper until the onions soften.
2. Add the basmati rice and stir to coat well.
3. Add the stock, coconut milk, thyme, turmeric and salt and bring to a boil.
4. Reduce the heat and simmer, covered for about 15-20 minutes.

GHANA
Vanilla Ice Cream

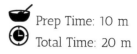 Prep Time: 10 m

Total Time: 20 m

Servings per Recipe: 4
Calories	94.7
Fat	0.3g
Cholesterol	0.0mg
Sodium	1.8mg
Carbohydrates	24.4g
Protein	1.0g

Ingredients
1 mango, peeled and finely chopped
2 bananas, peeled and sliced
2 tbsp lemon juice
4 tbsp orange juice
vanilla ice cream
cinnamon (optional)
brown sugar (optional)
peanuts (optional)

Directions
1. In a large bowl, mix together the mango and banana pieces.
2. Add the lemon and orange juice and gently, toss to coat.
3. With a scooper, place ice cream into a sundae dish and top with the mixed fruit evenly.
4. Serve with a sprinkling of the cinnamon and brown sugar.

Beef Bites
with Orangy Lentils Casserole

🥘 Prep Time: 1 hr
◉ Total Time: 2 hr

Servings per Recipe: 8	
Calories	796.4
Fat	36.3g
Cholesterol	133.8mg
Sodium	202.1mg
Carbohydrates	81.7g
Protein	40.6g

Ingredients

MEATBALLS
2 lbs minced beef
1 garlic clove, peeled & crushed
1 tsp ground cumin
1 tsp ground coriander
1 tsp cinnamon
1 large white onion, peeled & finely diced
1 egg, beaten
2 oz flour
Salt & pepper
2 tbsp olive oil
LENTILS
1 tbsp olive oil
1 garlic clove, peeled & crushed
1 white onion, peeled & diced
2 tsp ground cumin
2 tsp ground coriander
1 tsp cayenne pepper
4 oz split red lentils

16 oz chopped tomatoes
1 pint vegetable stock
1 cinnamon stick
8 oz no-soak whole dried apricots
1 lb cherry tomatoes, on the vine
CARAMELISED VEGETABLE ACCOMPANIMENT
2 tbsp olive oil
2 fennel bulbs, sliced, keep the fronds
2 white onions, peeled & quartered
4 carrots, peeled & cut into 1-inch chunks
2 oz brown sugar
3 fluid oz vegetable stock
1 orange, juice and zest of, grated
Salt & pepper
Fennel bulb, green fronds from
1 tsp fennel seed (optional)

Directions

1. Before you do anything preheat the oven to 360 F.
2. To prepare the meatballs:
3. Get a large mixing bowl: combine in it the garlic, cumin, coriander and cinnamon, salt & pepper.
4. Combine in the spices with onion and beaten egg. Stir them well. Shape the mix into small sized meatballs and place them on a lined baking sheet.
5. Place a large skillet over medium heat. Heat the oil in it. Cook in it the meatballs nit they become golden brown. Place them aside.
6. To prepare the lentils:

7. Place a large skillet over medium heat. Heat the oil in it. Sauté in it the onion with garlic for 3 min.
8. Stir in the spices with lentils and cook them for 1 min.
9. Combine in the tinned tomatoes, vegetable stock, cinnamon stick & the dried apricots. Let them cook for an extra 3 min.
10. Spoon the mix into a casserole dish then laid the meatballs on top with the cherry tomatoes. Cover the dish with a piece of foil.
11. Place the casserole in the oven and cook it for 65 min. discard the foil and cook it for another 10 min.
12. Place a large skillet over medium heat. Heat the oil in it. Sauté in it the onion with carrots and fennel bulb.
13. Cook them for 1 min. combine in the brown sugar then cook them over high heat until the sugar dissolves.
14. Lower the heat and stir in the stock. Put on the lid let them cook for 32 min.
15. Once the time is up, stir in the orange juice and cook them for 6 min uncovered.
16. Serve it with the lentils casserole warm.
17. Enjoy.

Creamy Marinated Grilled Kabobs

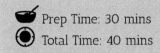

Prep Time: 30 mins
Total Time: 40 mins

Servings per Recipe: 4
Calories	210.4
Fat	6.9g
Cholesterol	72.9mg
Sodium	445.0mg
Carbohydrates	9.9g
Protein	26.7g

Ingredients

1/4 C. nonfat plain yogurt
1/4 C. chopped fresh parsley, plus
Extra parsley, for garnish
2 tbsp chopped fresh cilantro
2 tbsp lemon juice
1 tbsp extra virgin olive oil
3 garlic cloves, minced
1 1/2 tsp paprika (use a Smokey or regular variety)
1 tsp ground cumin
1/4 tsp ginger
1/2 tsp salt
1/4 tsp fresh ground pepper
1/8 tsp cayenne pepper
1 lb boneless skinless chicken breast, trimmed of fat and cut into 1 inch cubes
2 small red bell peppers cored, seeded and cut into 1 1/2-inch pieces
1 red onion, cut into large 1 inch pieces
1 medium zucchini, cut into 1/4-inch-thick rounds

Directions

1. Get a mixing bowl: whisk in it the yogurt, parsley, cilantro, lemon juice, oil, garlic, paprika, cumin, salt, pepper and cayenne.
2. Combine in the chicken pieces and stir them well. Cover the bowl with a piece of plastic wrap. Place it in the fridge for 30 min.
3. Before you do anything preheat the grill and grease its grates.
4. Bring a salted pot of water to a boil. Cook in it the bell peppers for 4 min. drain it and place it aside to dry.
5. Cook the zucchini in the same water for 1 min.
6. Thread the chicken pieces into skewers while alternating between it and the onion, pepper and zucchini pieces.
7. Grill the chicken kabobs for 4 to 6 min on each side. Serve them warm.
8. Enjoy.

TIPSY
Mango Shanks

Prep Time: 15 m
Total Time: 5 hr 15 m

Servings per Recipe: 4
Calories	847.3
Fat	41.3g
Cholesterol	242.7mg
Sodium	1374.8mg
Carbohydrates	39.3g
Protein	73.8g

Ingredients
4 lamb shanks
2 tbsp olive oil, divided use
1 onion, chopped finely
5 garlic cloves, crushed
1 tbsp cumin
2 tsp ground coriander
2 tsp cinnamon
3/4 tsp cayenne pepper
1 tsp grated fresh ginger

1/2 C. white wine
4 C. water
4 tsp instant chicken bouillon granules
1 tbsp tomato paste
4 tbsp honey
2 tbsp hot mango chutney
10 dried apricots, chopped finely
1 1/2 tbsp corn flour

Directions
1. Place a large skillet over medium heat. Heat 1 tbsp of oil in it. Brown in it the lamb shanks on both sides.

2. Place a large saucepan over medium heat. Heat the rest of oil in it. Add the garlic with onion and cook them for 3 min.

3. Stir in the cumin, coriander, cinnamon, cayenne and ginger. Cook them for 1 min.

4. Combine in the wine, water, stock granules, paste, honey and chutney. Cook them until they start boiling.

5. Stir in the lamb shanks a put on the lid. Lower the heat and cook them for 4 h on low while adding water if needed.

6. Stir in the apricots then cook them for an extra 12 min.

7. Whisk the corn flour with some water in a small bowl. Add it the pot and stir it gently.

8. Cook the stew until the broth thickens. Serve it warm.

9. Enjoy.

Acorn
Veggies and Raisins Stew

Prep Time: 10 mins
Total Time: 45 mins

Servings per Recipe: 6	
Calories	229.1
Fat	1.3g
Cholesterol	0.0mg
Sodium	459.5mg
Carbohydrates	51.4g
Protein	6.5g

Ingredients
1 large Spanish onion, diced
2 garlic cloves, minced
1 tsp turmeric
1/2 tsp curry powder
1/2 tsp cumin
1/4 tsp red pepper flakes
1/2 tsp salt
1/2 tsp pepper
3/4 tsp cinnamon
1/4 tsp ground nutmeg
2 sweet potatoes cut into 1 inch cubes

1 acorn squash, cut into 1 inch cubes
3 carrots cut into 1 inch rounds
1/2 C. vegetable broth
1 (15 oz) cans chickpeas, rinsed and drained
1 (15 oz) cans whole tomatoes
1/2 C. raisins

Directions
1. Place a pot over medium heat. Heat a splash of oil in it.
2. Add the onion with garlic for 3 min. stir in the spices and cook them for 1 min.
3. Combine in the carrot with potato, squash and broth. Cook them until they start boiling.
4. Lower the heat and cook the stew for 6 min. combine in the chick peas, tomatoes and raisins.
5. Put on the lid and cook them for 32 min until the veggies become tender. Serve your stew warm.
6. Enjoy.

TRADITIONAL
Rubbed Chicken Roast

Prep Time: 30 m
Total Time: 1 hr 30 m

Servings per Recipe: 4
Calories	848.9
Fat	64.6g
Cholesterol	243.8mg
Sodium	1114.9mg
Carbohydrates	7.7g
Protein	58.4g

Ingredients
1 whole chicken, about 4 lb
1 cinnamon stick, chopped in pieces
8 whole cloves
1 tsp cayenne
2 tsp cumin seeds
1 tsp fennel seed
1 tsp coriander seed
1 tbsp sweet paprika
1 1/2 tsp sea salt

1 tsp brown sugar
Sea salt & freshly ground black pepper, to taste
1 lemon, halved
1/4 bunch fresh cilantro
2 garlic cloves
3 tbsp extra-virgin olive oil

Directions
1. Before you do anything preheat the oven to 400 F.
2. Place a large pan over medium heat. Stir in it the cinnamon stick, cloves, cayenne, cumin, fennel, coriander and paprika. Cook them for 1 min.
3. Transfer the mix to a grinder and process them until they become finely ground.
4. Rub the mix into the chicken then season it with some salt and pepper. Place the garlic with lemon halves and cilantro inside of the chicken. Let it sit for 35 min.
5. Place the rubbed chicken in a roasting casserole dish then cook it in the oven for 1 h 10 min.
6. Once the time is up, wrap the chicken in a piece of foil then let it rest for 12 min. serve it warm.
7. Enjoy.

Cheesy Couscous
Stuffed Zucchini Boats

🥣 Prep Time: 10 mins
◉ Total Time: 45 mins

Servings per Recipe: 4
Calories   355.0
Fat   14.5g
Cholesterol   28.5mg
Sodium   435.5mg
Carbohydrates   43.3g
Protein   12.9g

Ingredients

2 zucchini, cut in half, lengthwise
2 tbsp olive oil
1 large onion, chopped
1 C. couscous
1 C. chicken stock
Basil leaves, chopped (small bunch)

4 oz feta cheese
Salt and pepper

Directions

1. Before you do anything preheat the oven to 350 F.
2. Lay the zucchini halves on a roasting pan. Cook it in the oven for 10 to 20 min or until it become golden brown with the cut up side facing down.
3. Use an ice cream spoon to scoop out the flesh of the zucchini into a bowl leaving skin as it is.
4. Place a large saucepan over medium heat. Heat the oil in it. Add the onion and cook it for 3 min.
5. Stir in the zucchini flesh with couscous, chicken stock and season with salt and pepper. Cook them until they start simmering.
6. Remove the saucepan from the heat and put on the lid. Place it aside to 6 min.
7. Fold the basil with feta cheese. Scoop the mix into the zucchini skin boats and place them on a lined up baking sheet.
8. Cook it in the oven for 5 min until it becomes golden brown. Serve it warm.
9. Enjoy.

SWEET LEMON
Chicken Stew

🥣 Prep Time: 30 m

🕐 Total Time: 6 hr 30 m

Servings per Recipe: 4
Calories	313.6
Fat	4.3g
Cholesterol	68.9mg
Sodium	516.6mg
Carbohydrates	44.5g
Protein	26.8g

Ingredients

4 carrots, peeled and sliced
2 large onions, halved and thinly sliced
2 lbs skinless chicken pieces
1/2 C. raisins
1/2 C. dried apricot, coarsely chopped
1 (14 oz) cans chicken broth
2 tbsp tomato paste
2 tbsp all-purpose flour
2 tbsp lemon juice

2 garlic cloves, minced
1 1/2 tsp ground cumin
1 1/2 tsp ground ginger
1 tsp ground cinnamon
Ground black pepper
Hot cooked couscous (whole wheat preferred)
Pine nuts, toasted
Fresh cilantro (optional)

Directions

1. Get a mixing bowl: mix in it the broth, tomato paste, flour, lemon juice, garlic, cumin, ginger, cinnamon and the ground black pepper.

2. Place the chicken in the slow cooker with carrots, onion and the broth mix.

3. Put on the lid and let it cook for 8 h on low. Once the time is up, serve it warm.

4. Enjoy.

Chickpeas
Mussels Stew

🥄 Prep Time: 15 mins
◉ Total Time: 45 mins

Servings per Recipe: 4	
Calories	590.5
Fat	19.6g
Cholesterol	95.5mg
Sodium	1728.0mg
Carbohydrates	55.7g
Protein	48.0g

Ingredients

1 medium onion, coarsely chopped
2 garlic cloves, thinly sliced
1 1/4 tsp ground cumin
1 tsp paprika (preferably hot)
1 tsp ground ginger
3/8 tsp ground cinnamon
1/8 tsp cayenne
3 tbsp olive oil
1 tbsp cider vinegar
1 (15 oz) cans chickpeas, drained and rinsed

2 tsp sugar
1 (28 oz) cans whole tomatoes with juice, juice reserved and tomatoes coarsely chopped
3 lbs mussels, scrubbed and beards removed
2 tbsp fresh flat-leaf parsley, chopped

Directions

1. Place a large pot over medium heat. Heat the oil in it. Add the garlic with onion and spices. Cook them for 7 min.
2. Combine in the vinegar and cook them for 2 min.
3. Stir in the tomato with sugar and chickpeas. Cook them for 16 min over medium heat.
4. Stir the mussels into the pot. Put on the lid and let them cook for 7 min. serve your mussels stew warm.
5. Enjoy.

SHISH VEGGIES
Lamb Kebab

Prep Time: 20 m
Total Time: 35 m

Servings per Recipe: 6

Calories	505.2
Fat	28.5g
Cholesterol	109.6mg
Sodium	120.2mg
Carbohydrates	30.1g
Protein	33.6g

Ingredients
8 oz plain yogurt
2 tbsp lemon juice
1 tsp olive oil
1 large onion, minced
1/2 C. chopped mint leaf
2 tbsp chopped fresh cilantro or 2 tbsp fresh parsley
Salt and pepper
1/4 tsp cayenne pepper

2 lbs boneless leg of lamb or 2 lbs beef sirloin, cut into cubes
18 cherry tomatoes
2 green peppers cut into chunks
18 small white onions, peeled
18 medium mushrooms

Directions
1. Get a large mixing bowl: whisk in it the yogurt, lemon juice, olive oil, onion, mint, cilantro, salt, pepper and cayenne pepper.
2. Add the lamb pieces and stir them well. Cover the bowl with a piece of plastic wrap. Place it in the fridge for 6 to 8 h.
3. Before you do anything preheat the grill and grease its grates.
4. Drain the meat from the marinade. Thread it into skewers with mushroom, onion, cherry tomatoes and peppers.
5. Grill the kabobs for 4 to 7 min on each side. Serve them warm.
6. Enjoy.

Cinnamon
Lentils Soup

🥄 Prep Time: 15 mins
◉ Total Time: 45 mins

Servings per Recipe: 4
Calories	311.8
Fat	1.0g
Cholesterol	0.0mg
Sodium	322.5mg
Carbohydrates	56.8g
Protein	19.8g

Ingredients
7 C. hot water
1 1/2 C. dried brown lentils
3 C. chopped onions
2 tsp instant beef bouillon
1 1/2 tsp cumin
3/4 tsp sugar
1/2 tsp salt

1/2 tsp cinnamon
1/4 tsp allspice
1/4 tsp ground red pepper (optional)

Directions
1. Place a large pot over medium heat.
2. Pour the water into it and cook it until it starts boiling. Stir in the lentils and bring them to a boil.
3. Lower the heat and cook it for 12 min.
4. Place a large skillet over medium heat. Grease it with a cooking spray. Sauté the onion in it for 9 min.
5. Stir the mix into the pot with lentils. Put on the lid and cook the soup for 25 min over low heat. Serve it warm.
6. Enjoy.

HARISSA
Seared Lamb Fillets

Prep Time: 8 m
Total Time: 18 m

Servings per Recipe: 2
Calories	151.1
Fat	14.1g
Cholesterol	0.0mg
Sodium	4.5mg
Carbohydrates	7.3g
Protein	0.8g

Ingredients
2 - 3 lamb fillets (blackstrap)
1 tsp ground cumin
1 tsp paprika
3 garlic cloves, crushed
1 tsp ground coriander
1 tsp dried parsley flakes
1/2 tsp cinnamon
1/2 tsp ground ginger
1 tsp sugar

1/2 tsp harissa, see appendix
2 tbsp lemon juice
2 tbsp olive oil

Directions
1. Combine the spices with garlic, olive oil and lemon juice in a large mixing bowl. Whisk them well.
2. Add the lamb fillets to the bowl and stir them to coat.
3. Place a large skillet over medium heat. Heat a splash of oil in it.
4. Cook in it the lamb fillets for 4 to 6 min on each see or until they are done. Serve them warm.
5. Enjoy.

Herbed
Fava Beans

Prep Time: 15 mins
Total Time: 20 mins

Servings per Recipe: 4
Calories   144.9
Fat   5.5g
Cholesterol   7.6mg
Sodium   27.8mg
Carbohydrates   17.9g
Protein   6.8g

Ingredients

12 oz. frozen fava beans
1 tbsp butter
4 -5 scallions, sliced
1 tbsp chopped fresh cilantro
1 tsp chopped of fresh mint

1/2-1 tsp ground cumin
2 tsps olive oil
salt

Directions

1. In a pan of water, cook the fava beans for about 3-4 minutes and drain well.
2. Keep aside to cool.
3. Peel off the outer skin of the fava beans and keep aside.
4. In a pan, melt the butter and sauté the scallions for about 2-3 minutes.
5. Stir in the fava beans, fresh herbs and a pinch of salt.
6. Stir in the olive oil and remove it from heat.
7. Serve immediately.

PECAN
Couscous Salad

Prep Time: 15 m
Total Time: 25 m

Servings per Recipe: 6

Calories	211.9
Fat	11.3g
Cholesterol	0.0mg
Sodium	197.9mg
Carbohydrates	23.7g
Protein	4.3g

Ingredients

6 oz instant couscous
2 tbsp lemon juice (or to taste)
3 tbsp olive oil
1/2 tsp salt
1/8 tsp white pepper
1/4 C. finely chopped of fresh mint
1/3 C. chopped pecans, toasted if desired

Directions

1. Cook the couscous by following the instructions on the package.

2. Transfer the couscous to a mixing bowl. Stir in the rest of the ingredients then serve it.

3. Enjoy.

Oven-Seared
Spiced Beef

Prep Time: 10 mins

Total Time: 25 mins

Servings per Recipe: 4
Calories	64.8
Fat	7.0g
Cholesterol	0.0mg
Sodium	12.2mg
Carbohydrates	0.8g
Protein	0.2g

Ingredients
4 (6 oz.) filet of beef
1 tsp coriander seed, crushed
1/2 tsp white peppercorns, crushed
1 tsp dried ancho chile powder
1 tsp ground cumin

2 tbsp olive oil
salt

Directions
1. Set your oven to 375 degrees F before doing anything else.
2. Heat a large ovenproof skillet on high heat.
3. In a large bowl, mix together all the ingredients except the beef and oil.
4. Add the beef mixture and coat it with the spice mixture generously.
5. In the heated skillet add the oil and then place the beef fillets.
6. Transfer the skillet into the oven and sear everything for about 4-6 minutes per side.
7. Remove from the oven and cut into desired size slices.
8. Serve with a topping of your choice

EGGS
in Spicy Tomato Sauce

Prep Time: 10 m

Total Time: 35 m

Servings per Recipe: 4

Calories	192.3
Fat	9.2g
Cholesterol	211.5mg
Sodium	665.1mg
Carbohydrates	20.1g
Protein	9.7g

Ingredients

For four people
4 big ripe tomatoes
4 eggs
2 sweet peppers
2 medium onions, chopped
1 - 2 hot green pepper
1 head garlic, all cloves crushed and cut
1 tbsp tomato concentrate
1 tbsp harissa

1 tbsp cumin
bay leaf
thyme, to taste
salt, to taste
1 - 4 tbsp olive oil

Directions

1. Remove the seeds of the peppers and chop them.
2. Cut the tomatoes into large pieces.
3. In a medium pan, heat the oil and sauté the onion and garlic till soft.
4. Stir in the cumin and sauté for a few mins.
5. Stir in the remaining ingredients except eggs and cook till vegetables are done.
6. With a spoon, make 4 wells in the veggie mixture and carefully crack 1 egg in each well.
7. Cover the pan and cook for about 15 minutes.
8. Serve with the bread of your choice.

Hot Sausages & Eggs

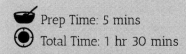
Prep Time: 5 mins
Total Time: 1 hr 30 mins

Servings per Recipe: 4
Calories	374.9
Fat	17.8g
Cholesterol	279.0mg
Sodium	152.7mg
Carbohydrates	40.5g
Protein	14.4g

Ingredients

3 - 4 tbsp olive oil
4 medium potatoes, cubed
1 - 2 tbsp tomato paste
1 - 4 tsp harissa, diluted in a little water
3 - 4 garlic cloves, skinned and crushed
2 - 3 dried chilies, seeded and coarsely chopped
2 tsps crushed caraway seeds
2 tsps paprika
6 small spicy sausage, sliced
6 eggs
salt

Directions

1. In a large pan, heat the oil and fry the potatoes lightly.
2. Stir in the harissa, tomato paste, chilies, garlic, caraway seeds, paprika and enough water that covers the mixture and cook for about 45 minutes on low heat.
3. Stir in sausage and simmer for about 15 minutes.
4. In a bowl, beat the eggs and slowly, add in the pan, stirring continuously till eggs sets to a firm but creamy consistency.
5. Stir in salt and serve immediately.

BAKED
Veggie Omelet

🍳 Prep Time: 15 m
🕐 Total Time: 1 hr 35 m

Servings per Recipe: 6
Calories	230.6
Fat	15.0g
Cholesterol	268.8mg
Sodium	360.9mg
Carbohydrates	8.8g
Protein	15.5g

Ingredients

1 (1-1 1/2 lb.) eggplant
1 tbsp extra virgin olive oil
1 medium onion, finely chopped
1 medium red bell pepper, diced
8 large eggs, beaten
1/2 bunch flat leaf parsley, minced
2 garlic cloves, minced

1/4 tsp rose water
1/2 tsp salt
1/4 tsp fresh ground pepper
1/8 tsp ground cinnamon
1 tsp harissa, dissolved in 1 tbsp of water
1/4 lb gruyere cheese, grated

Directions

1. Set your oven to 450 degrees F before doing anything else and line a baking sheet with greased foil paper.
2. Cut the eggplant in half lengthwise and then score down the center without cutting through the skin.
3. Arrange the eggplant onto the prepared baking sheet, cut side down.
4. Cook everything in the oven for about 20 minutes and remove from the oven then keep aside to cool.
5. Now, set your oven to 350 degrees F.
6. After cooling, peel and chop the eggplant.
7. In a nonstick skillet, heat 1 tbsp of the oil on medium heat and cook the bell pepper and onion for about 5-10 minutes, stirring occasionally.
8. Stir in the eggplant, garlic and a pinch of salt and cook for about 1 minute and remove from heat.
9. In a large bowl, add beaten eggs, parsley, harissa, rose water, cinnamon, salt and black pepper and mix well then stir in cheese and eggplant.
10. In a large greased baking dish, place the eggplant mixture evenly and cook it in the oven for about 30 minutes.
11. Remove the dish from the oven and keep aside to cool for about 10 minutes.
12. Cut into desired size wedges and serve.

BAKED
Lamb & Veggie Stew

Prep Time: 20 m
Total Time: 3 hr 35 m

Servings per Recipe: 4

Calories	933.8
Fat	40.6g
Cholesterol	120.0mg
Sodium	923.9mg
Carbohydrates	89.4g
Protein	62.1g

Ingredients

2 lbs lamb, cut in 2 inch pieces
3 lbs artichokes
3 lbs canned green peas
1 tsp ginger
1 pinch saffron
1 clove garlic
3 tbsp olive oil

1 preserved lemon
1/2 lb black olives
1 bunch parsley
lemon juice

Directions

1. Set your oven to 300 degrees F before doing anything else.
2. In a heatproof pan, mix together the ginger, garlic, saffron and 2 tbsp of the olive oil.
3. Add the lamb and coat with the mixture evenly.
4. Place 1 tbsp of the oil in the center of the ginger mixture and then place the meat on top.
5. Clean the artichokes, then remove the leaves and core it. (Only use the heart)
6. Place the artichoke over the meat evenly.
7. Skin the preserved lemons.
8. Place the olives over the artichoke, followed by the skin of the preserved lemon.
9. With your hands, squeeze the pulp of the lemon on top and then add 1/2 C. of water.
10. Cook everything in the oven for about 2 1/2 hours, checking after every 45 minutes.
11. Add the green peas and cook for about 10 minutes more.
12. Serve this stew with the couscous.

ALMONDS & ORANGE
Pastries

Prep Time: 30 m
Total Time: 35 m

Servings per Recipe: 4
Calories   807.5
Fat   40.3g
Cholesterol   0.0mg
Sodium   500.1mg
Carbohydrates   97.9g
Protein   19.0g

Ingredients
2/3 C. sugar
1 1/4 C. water
1 tbsp lemon juice
1 tbsp orange flower water
1 1/2 C. blanched almonds, lightly toasted and ground
1 1/2 tsps finely grated orange peel

1 1/2 tsps ground cinnamon
4 oz. phyllo pastry
2 tbsp olive oil, for brushing
lightly toasted sesame seeds, for sprinkling

Directions
1. In a pan, add 1/2 cup of the sugar and water on medium heat and stir till dissolved completely.
2. Add the lemon juice and bring to a boil and cook till a syrup forms.
3. Remove everything from the heat and stir in the orange flower water and remove from heat and let it cool completely.
4. Set your oven to 350 degrees F.
5. For the filling, in a blender, add the orange peel, remaining sugar, ground almonds and cinnamon and pulse till well combined.
6. Place the phyllo sheets under a damp cloth before using.
7. Coat 1 phyllo sheet with olive oil and then cut into 3 strips lengthwise.
8. Place about 1 spoonful of the filling mixture over the bottom of each strip.
9. Fold the sides of each strip over the filling and then roll the strip along the length.
10. With oil, brush the inside and seal to secure the filling.
11. Repeat with the remaining phyllo sheets and the filling.
12. Coat the pastries with the oil and arrange onto a large baking sheet in a single layer.
13. Cook everything in the oven for about 15-20 minutes.
14. Remove the pastries from the oven and soak in the syrup for about 3 minutes.
15. Transfer the pastries onto serving platters and sprinkle with sesame seeds generously.
16. Keep aside to cool before serving.

Herbed Potato Pastries

🥄 Prep Time: 30 mins
◉ Total Time: 1 hr 10 mins

Servings per Recipe: 48
Calories   35.9
Fat   0.5g
Cholesterol   5.1mg
Sodium   101.8mg
Carbohydrates   6.6g
Protein   1.1g

Ingredients

1 lb russet potato, peeled and cut into 1 inch chunks
1 onion, peeled and chopped
2 cloves garlic, peeled and minced
1 tbsp olive oil
3 tbsp minced parsley
3 tbsp minced fresh cilantro

1 tbsp drained capers, rinsed and coarsely chopped
1 tsp salt
1/2 tsp fresh ground pepper
1 large egg, separated
12 egg roll wraps (6-inch squares)
vegetable oil (for frying)

Directions

1. In a pan of salted water, cook the potatoes for about 15 minutes and drain well.
2. In a bowl, place the potatoes and with a potato masher, mash them.
3. In a frying pan, heat the oil on medium heat and sauté the onion and garlic for about 10 minutes.
4. Stir in the mashed potatoes, capers, fresh herbs, salt and black pepper.
5. In a bowl, beat the egg yolks well and stir into the potato mixture and remove from heat.
6. In another small bowl, beat the egg whites.
7. Cut each egg roll into 4 equal sized squares and cover with plastic wrap before serving.
8. Divide the potato mixture over each square evenly.
9. With egg whites, brush the edges of each square and fold diagonally over filling to form a triangle.
10. With your fingers, pinch the edges to seal.
11. In a large pan, heat about 2-inches of the oil on medium heat to 375 degrees F.
12. Fry the pastries in batches for about 3-5 minutes, turning once.
13. Transfer the pastries onto some paper towel lined plates to drain.

NORTH AFRICAN
Breakfast Eggs

Prep Time: 10 m
Total Time: 3 h 10 m

Servings per Recipe: 4
Calories	164.4
Fat	13.3g
Cholesterol	215.3mg
Sodium	401.0mg
Carbohydrates	4.6g
Protein	6.9g

Ingredients
2 roma tomatoes, diced
1/2 C. , frozen tri-colored bell pepper strips thawed
2 tbsps extra virgin olive oil
1/2 C. onion, sliced thinly
1 medium garlic clove, minced
1 tsp paprika
1/2 tbsp of cold unsalted butter

3/4 tsp kosher salt, to taste
1 tsp fresh black pepper
4 large eggs, room temperature
2 tsps flat-leaf Italian parsley, chopped

Directions
1. In a large bowl, add the peppers, tomatoes, 1 tbsp of the oil, salt and black pepper and toss to coat.
2. In another bowl, mix together the onions, garlic, remaining oil, paprika, salt and black pepper and toss to coat.
3. In a 9-inch round cake pan, place the peppers mixture on one side and the onion mixture on the other side.
4. Place the butter on top of both mixtures.
5. Arrange the pan into a slow cooker and slow cook for about 2 hours.
6. With a spatula, stir all the ingredients in the pan till well combined and slowly cook for about 1 hour more.
7. With a wooden spoon, make 4 wells in the vegetable mixture.
8. Crack the eggs, one at a time in a small bowl and sprinkle with salt and black pepper.
9. Carefully, place 1 egg in each well and slow cook for about 25-30 minutes more.
10. Serve with a garnishing of parsley alongside the rice or bread.

Spicy
Roasted Chicken

Prep Time: 5 mins
Total Time: 1 hr 25 mins

Servings per Recipe: 4
Calories   305.9
Fat   23.1g
Cholesterol   100.3mg
Sodium   132.1mg
Carbohydrates   2.5g
Protein   21.6g

Ingredients
1 chicken
1 lemon
2 garlic cloves, crushed
1 bunch thyme
2 tbsps butter

1/2 tbsp ground cumin
1/2 tbsp ground coriander

Directions
1. Set your oven to 375 degrees F before doing anything else.
2. In a bowl, mix together the garlic, butter, spices and salt.
3. With your fingers, loosen the skin under the breast and thighs.
4. With your fingers rub the butter mixture under the skin and over the skin evenly and drizzle with lemon juice.
5. Stuff the cavity of the chicken with thyme bunch and lemon halves.
6. Sprinkle the chicken with the salt and black pepper generously.
7. Arrange the chicken into prepared roasting pan, breast side down.
8. Cook in the oven for about 80-90 minutes.

NORTH AFRICAN
Lamb with Sauce

Prep Time: 15 m
Total Time: 50 m

Servings per Recipe: 4

Calories	382.7
Fat	17.2g
Cholesterol	741.9mg
Sodium	427.9mg
Carbohydrates	13.8g
Protein	42.3g

Ingredients
800 g fresh lamb liver
6 -8 garlic cloves, minced
2 C. chopped tinned tomatoes with juice
1/2 C. chopped fresh coriander
2 -3 tsps fresh ground cumin
salt & freshly ground black pepper
1 C. water
2 tbsps good quality olive oil

Directions
1. Cut the lamb liver into 1-inch long and 1/2-inch wide pieces.
2. In large frying pan, heat the oil on medium heat and stir fry the liver till browned from all sides.
3. Increase the heat to medium-high and sauté the garlic and cumin for a while.
4. Meanwhile in a blender, pulse the tomatoes with juice till a fine puree forms.
5. In the pan, stir in tomato puree, water, salt and black pepper and cook, covered for about 25 minutes.
6. Stir in half of the coriander and remove from heat.
7. Serve with a garnishing of the remaining coriander alongside your desired side dish.

Chicken
and Chickpeas

🥣 Prep Time: 20 mins
◉ Total Time: 1 hr 25 mins

Servings per Recipe: 6	
Calories	332.8
Fat	13.5g
Cholesterol	53.9mg
Sodium	962.1mg
Carbohydrates	41.6g
Protein	12.2g

Ingredients
2 tbsps oil
1/2 C. onion, chopped
1 lb skinless chicken piece, rid of fat and skin
10 sprigs flat leaf parsley, leaves only, chopped
1/4 C. chickpeas, cooked

1 tsp black pepper
1 tsp salt
1/2 tsp cinnamon
3 C. water
2 lbs frozen french fries
1 egg, beaten
lemon wedge, for serving

Directions
1. In a pan, heat the oil on low heat and stir in the chicken, chickpeas, onion, half of the parsley, cinnamon and salt.
2. Cover and simmer, stirring occasionally for about 10 minutes.
3. Stir in the water and bring to a boil on medium heat.
4. Cook for about 40 minutes.
5. Meanwhile, cook the French fries according to package's instructions.
6. Stir in the beaten egg and French fries in the pan and simmer for about 10 minutes more.
7. Serve with a garnishing of the remaining parsley.

GARBANZO BEANS
and Veggie Soup

Prep Time: 20 m
Total Time: 55 m

Servings per Recipe: 1
Calories	138.6
Fat	3.9g
Cholesterol	0.0mg
Sodium	434.6mg
Carbohydrates	23.7g
Protein	3.5g

Ingredients
1 onion
2 garlic cloves
2 tbsps cilantro
2 tbsps olive oil
2 carrots, cut into large pieces
1 large potato, cut into large pieces
1 1/2 C. butternut squash, cut into large pieces
2 tbsps tomato paste
1 C. garbanzo beans

2 tbsps bulgher wheat
8 C. water
1 tsp salt
pepper, to taste
1 tsp paprika
1 pinch cayenne (optional)

Directions
1. In a skillet, heat the oil and sauté onion and garlic till tender.
2. Stir in the vegetables, cilantro and spices and then pour in water.
3. Simmer, covered on medium heat for about 15 minutes.
4. Transfer the vegetables into a large bowl and with a hand blender, mash them.
5. In the same pan, add the mashed vegetables with beans, bulgur wheat and tomato paste and simmer for about 10 - 15 minutes more.

Almond
Baklawa

🥘 Prep Time: 1 hr
⏱ Total Time: 2 hr 25 mins

Servings per Recipe: 20
Calories   545.7
Fat   36.0g
Cholesterol   35.6mg
Sodium   231.2mg
Carbohydrates   51.3g
Protein   8.0g

Ingredients

24 oz. plain flour
310 ml water
200 ml melted ghee mixed with 110ml sunflower oil
1/2 tsp salt
18 oz. chopped almonds
128 g granulated sugar

1/4 tsp ground cinnamon
1 tsp vanilla sugar
2 tsps melted ghee
155 ml orange flower water (mazhar)
310 - 620 ml honey
155 - 310 ml orange flower water (mazhar)
310 ml extra of melted ghee

Directions

1. Set your oven to 300 degrees F before doing anything else and grease a large tray with a little melted ghee.
2. In a bowl, mix together the flour, salt and ghee/oil mixture.
3. Slowly, add the water and mix till a smooth dough forms.
4. Dust a smooth surface with the corn flour.
5. Divide the dough into 2 portions and place one onto floured surface, covered with a kitchen towel.
6. Shape another portion into golf sized balls.
7. Roll the balls into sausage shapes and again roll on a floured surface into a 3-4 mm thickness.
8. With a little corn flour, dust the dough sheets and process in the pasta machine on the lowest settings for thinnest strips.
9. Arrange the first strip vertically in the center of prepared tray and coat with ghee.
10. Place a second strip horizontally over the first strip.
11. Repeat with the remaining strips and ghee, covering the tray completely in 5 layers. (There should be 5 strips in each layer)
12. For filling in a food processor, add the almonds and pulse till chopped finely.
13. Transfer the almonds into a bowl with the sugar, vanilla sugar, cinnamon and mazhar and mix till well combined.

14. Place the filling over strips evenly in the tray and with a spatula, smooth the surface gently.
15. Roll the other dough portion and make golf size balls.
16. Roll the ball into sausage shape and again roll onto floured surface into 3 - 4 mm thickness.
17. With a little corn flour, dust the dough sheets and process in the pasta machine on the lowest settings for thinnest strips.
18. Place the strips over filling in the same process you have for the first portion. (This time you should have 6 layers of strips)
19. With a knife, cut the straight vertical lines all the way to bottom and then cut more lines diagonally to make diamond shape.
20.   Press a whole almond in the center of each diamond.
21. Cook in the oven for about 60 - 70 minutes.
22. For syrup in a pan, warm the mazhar and honey.
23. Remove the baking tray from the oven and pour the syrup over the baklawa and keep aside for at least 10 minutes.
24. Cut into desired pieces and serve.

Semolina
Flatbread

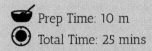 Prep Time: 10 m

Total Time: 25 mins

Servings per Recipe: 8
Calories   209.9
Fat   7.1g
Cholesterol   0.0mg
Sodium   873.5mg
Carbohydrates   30.4g
Protein   5.2g

Ingredients
2 C. semolina flour
1 tbsp salt
1/4 C. olive oil
1 C. water

Directions
1. In a bowl, mix together all the ingredients except water.
2. Slowly, add the water and mix till a soft dough forms.
3. Make 2 equal sized balls from dough and flatten onto lightly floured surface to your desired size.
4. Heat a frying pan on medium heat and cook from both sides till golden brown.
5. Cut into desired size wedges before serving.

FISH
Veggie Soup

Prep Time: 15 m
Total Time: 55 m

Servings per Recipe: 6
Calories	402.5
Fat	11.0g
Cholesterol	91.6mg
Sodium	270.3mg
Carbohydrates	33.4g
Protein	42.5g

Ingredients
1 kg fish fillet
2 large potatoes
2 green bell peppers
1 large carrot
1 fennel bulb
2 onions
1 celery rib
4 tbsps tomato paste
2 liters water
1 tbsp cumin

1 tsp ras el hanout spice mix
1 tsp coriander
2 bay leaves
1 piece lemon rind
1 tbsp harissa
4 tbsps olive oil

Directions
1. Chop the onion and then sauté in heated oil till golden in a large soup pan.
2. Chop all the vegetables and cook in the pan till soft.
3. Stir in the tomato paste and cook for a few seconds.
4. Add the water, lemon rind and spices and bring to a boil.
5. Reduce the heat to low and simmer for about 20 minutes.
6. Cut the fish into cubes and stir in the soup.
7. Simmer for about 15 minutes more.
8. With a hand blender, puree the soup to the desired consistency.
9. Serve with the baguette bread and lemon slices.

Spicy
Eggplant

Prep Time: 10 m
Total Time: 30 mins

Servings per Recipe: 6
Calories	43.0
Fat	0.4g
Cholesterol	0.0mg
Sodium	4.3mg
Carbohydrates	10.0g
Protein	1.7g

Ingredients
2 eggplants
2 garlic cloves, crushed
1 tsp sweet paprika
1 1/2 tsps cumin, ground

1/2 tsp sugar
1 tbsp lemon juice

Directions
1. Cut the eggplant into 1/2-inch slices and place in a colander.
2. Sprinkle with salt and keep aside for about 20 minutes to drain.
3. Rinse well and gently squeeze, then pat dry.
4. In a large frying pan, heat about 1/4-inch of the oil on medium heat and fry the eggplant slices in batches till golden brown from both sides.
5. Transfer the eggplant slices onto a paper towel lined plate to drain and then chop them finely.
6. In a bowl, add the chopped eggplant slices with garlic, sugar, cumin and paprika.
7. With a paper towel, wipe the frying pan and place it on medium heat.
8. Add the eggplant mixture and cook, stirring continuously for about 2 minutes.
9. Serve with a drizzling of lemon juice.

SPICY LAMB
Sausage

Prep Time: 35 m
Total Time: 35 m

Servings per Recipe: 1
Calories	306.9
Fat	22.5g
Cholesterol	78.1mg
Sodium	306.6mg
Carbohydrates	5.8g
Protein	19.9g

Ingredients
2 lbs boneless lamb, cut into 2 inch pieces
4 oz. lamb fat attached to the lamb kidney
2 heads garlic, about 12 cloves, peeled
1 tsp salt (to taste)
1 tsp black pepper
1 tbsp ground cumin
1 tbsp ground coriander

1 tbsp sumac
1 tbsp red hot chili powder
2 tbsps sweet paprika
1 C. cold water
1 small lamb intestine casing

Directions
1. In a grinder, add the lamb, fat from lamb kidneys, and garlic and grind well.
2. Add the remaining ingredients except casing and grind till well combined.
3. Make mini patties from the mixture and fry each patty in a little oil.
4. Tightly, tie the one side of the casing.
5. In the casing add the lamb mixture and twist after every 4-inches to divide into individual sausages.
6. Fry these sausages in vegetable oil till golden brown.

Almond Bread with Orange Blossom Syrup

Prep Time: 20 m
Total Time: 1 h 30 m

Servings per Recipe: 15
Calories   348.8
Fat   18.8g
Cholesterol   101.0mg
Sodium   194.5mg
Carbohydrates   43.2g
Protein   4.3g

Ingredients

1 C. egg
1 C. sugar
1 C. butter
1 C. of freshly ground almonds
1 C. stale bread
1 1/2 tsps baking powder
1 lemon, zest of, large

1/2 tsp vanilla essence
For the Syrup
2 C. granulated sugar
4 C. water
1 1/2 tbsps orange blossom water (mazhar)

Directions

1. Set your oven to 375 degrees F before doing anything else.
2. For Syrup, in a pan, mix together the water and sugar and boil for about 10-15 minutes.
3. Stir in the mazhar in the last couple of minutes.
4. Remove from heat and let it cool slightly.
5. In a bowl, crack the eggs and beat till fluffy.
6. Add butter and sugar and beat till well combined and then fold in remaining ingredients.
7. Transfer the mixture into a round metal tin and with the back of a spatula, smooth the surface.
8. Cook in the oven for about 40 minutes or till a toothpick inserted in the center comes out clean.
9. Remove from the oven and pour the sugar syrup over bread.
10. Cut the bread into desired slices and serve.

SPICED
Flatbread

Prep Time: 50 m
Total Time: 54 m

Servings per Recipe: 1
Calories	183.4
Fat	9.8g
Cholesterol	0.0mg
Sodium	195.9mg
Carbohydrates	21.8g
Protein	4.0g

Ingredients
3 C. finely ground whole wheat flour
1 tsp salt
1/2 C. olive oil, divided
1 1/2 C. water
1 tsp ground cumin
1 tsp sweet paprika
1 tsp turmeric

Directions
1. For dough in a large bowl, mix together 2 tbsps of the oil, flour and salt.
2. Slowly, add the required amount of the water and mix till a soft dough forms.
3. Place the dough onto a floured surface and knead for about 15 minutes. (Dust with a little flour while kneading)
4. Make a ball from the dough and brush with 2 tbsps of oil.
5. Place the dough ball in a bowl and with a plastic wrap, cover the bowl.
6. Keep aside in the warm place for about 1 hour.
7. In a small bowl, mix together the remaining 1/4 C. of oil and spices.
8. For the flatbread divide the dough into 12 equal sized balls and flatten the each ball into a disk.
9. Place the disks, one at a time onto a lightly floured surface and with a rolling pin, roll the each disk thinly into a 9-inch round.
10. With your fingertips, spread about 1 tsp of spiced oil over each flat bread and tightly roll up into a long cylinder and then coil into a tight spiral.
11. Place one flatbread onto a large parchment paper and cover with plastic wrap.
12. Place the remaining flatbreads in the same way.
13. Arrange a parchment paper onto a smooth surface and roll each spiral into 6-inches round.
14. Heat a large cast-iron skillet on medium heat and cook each flatbread for about 3-4 minutes, turning once.

Semolina Pancakes

🍳 Prep Time: 10 m
⏱ Total Time: 40 m

Servings per Recipe: 6

Calories	444.7
Fat	6.8g
Cholesterol	104.3mg
Sodium	225.8mg
Carbohydrates	77.3g
Protein	18.4g

Ingredients

2 C. fine semolina
1 C. plain flour
1 C. whole wheat flour
3 eggs
2 tsps baking powder
1 tbsp instant yeast
2 tsps sugar

1 pinch salt
1 C. warm water
2 C. milk
1 tbsp vegetable oil (optional)

Directions

1. In a large bowl, mix together the flours, semolina, eggs, yeast, sugar, baking powder and salt.
2. Slowly, add the milk and water and mix till a thick but runny mixture forms.
3. In a frying pan, heat a little oil and add the desired amount of the mixture and tilt the pan to coat the bottom.
4. Cook on both sides till desired doneness.

DRIED
Fruit Balls

Prep Time: 5 m
Total Time: 5 m

Servings per Recipe: 1
Calories   192.7
Fat   0.6g
Cholesterol   0.0mg
Sodium   7.2mg
Carbohydrates   46.6g
Protein   2.2g

Ingredients
1 3/4 C. pitted prunes, chopped
1 3/4 C. dried figs
1/4 C. sweet red wine
1 tsp cinnamon
1/4 tsp nutmeg
2 tbsps confectioners' sugar

Directions
1. In a large food processor, add all the ingredients and pulse till a smooth mixture forms.
2. Roll into walnut sized balls and serve. (For better result you can mix in 1 C. of almonds)

Egyptian Cream Pudding

Prep Time: 5 m
Total Time: 15 m

Servings per Recipe: 4
Calories   205.4
Fat   8.9g
Cholesterol   25.6mg
Sodium   117.8mg
Carbohydrates   24.7g
Protein   7.3g

Ingredients

3 tbsp finely ground rice
3 C. milk
2 1/2 tbsp sugar

1 tbsp rose water
2 tbsp mixed nuts, chopped

Directions

1. Get a mixing bowl: Stir in it 1 C. of milk with rice.
2. Place a large saucepan over medium heat: Combine in it the milk with sugar. Cook them until they start boiling. Add the rice and milk mix. Stir them.
3. Reduce the heat and cook the pudding until it becomes thick. Turn off the heat and add the rosewater. Serve your pudding with some nuts.
4. Enjoy.

EGYPTIAN
Walla-Walla Salad

Prep Time: 1 h
Total Time: 1 h

Servings per Recipe: 4

Calories	380.8
Fat	32.7g
Cholesterol	80.2mg
Sodium	1008.6mg
Carbohydrates	9.7g
Protein	13.5g

Ingredients

1 large English cucumber, peeled, halved
lengthwise
salt
12 oz feta cheese
1/2 C. finely chopped walla-walla onion
1/4 C. fresh lemon juice
1/4 C. olive oil

fresh ground pepper
2 tbsp fresh mint sprigs

Directions

1. Pierce the cucumber several times with a fork. Season it with some salt and place it aside for 22 min.
2. Get a serving bowl: Mash the cheese slightly with your hand. Add the onion, lemon juice and oil, a pinch of salt and pepper. Mix them well with a fork.
3. Rinse the cucumber with some cool water. Pat it dry and slice it. Add it to the cheese mix and stir them.
4. Chill the salad in the fridge for 32 min then serve it.
5. Enjoy.

Cauliflower
in Spicy Sauce

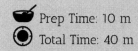

Prep Time: 10 m
Total Time: 40 m

Servings per Recipe: 4
Calories   171.1
Fat   13.8g
Cholesterol   0.0mg
Sodium   628.3mg
Carbohydrates   11.0g
Protein   3.6g

Ingredients

8 oz. tomatoes, chopped
2 large garlic cloves, finely chopped
4 tbsps olive oil
1 tsp paprika
1 tsp salt
1 tsp black pepper
1 tsp harissa

1 cauliflower, medium sized, trimmed, cut into florets

Directions

1. In a pan of salted water, cook the cauliflower for about 7-8 minutes.
2. Drain the cauliflower well, reserving some cooking liquid.
3. Meanwhile in another pan, heat the oil and sauté the garlic for about 1 minute.
4. Stir in the remaining ingredients and reduce the heat to low.
5. Simmer the sauce for about 10 minutes and stir in the cauliflower.
6. Simmer, stirring occasionally for about 5 minutes. (Use reserved water if sauce is to thick)
7. Serve this dish over boiled rice with a garnishing of parsley.

EGYPTIAN
Veggies Omelet

Prep Time: 10 m
Total Time: 20 m

Servings per Recipe: 4
Calories	292.3
Fat	24.6g
Cholesterol	317.2mg
Sodium	108.8mg
Carbohydrates	7.8g
Protein	10.4g

Ingredients
6 eggs
1 tbsp flour
salt & pepper
1 large onion, diced
5 tbsp oil
1/2 bunch parsley, chopped semi fine
1 tomatoes, diced
1/2 green bell pepper, diced

Directions
1. Before you do anything preheat the oven broiler.
2. Get a mixing bowl: Whisk in it the eggs with pepper, flour, a pinch of salt and pepper.
3. Place a large skillet over medium heat. Heat 2 tbsp of oil in it. Add the onion and cook it for 3 min.
4. Stir in the tomato with parsley, and pepper for 4 min. Turn off the heat and let them lose heat. Add the beaten eggs and stir them well.
5. Coat an ovenproof pan with the rest of the oil. Place it over medium heat and heat it. Spread the eggs and veggies mix in it.
6. Cook it for 3 to 5 min or until the omelet is set on the bottom. Transfer the pan to the oven and broil it for 4 min. Serve it warm.
7. Enjoy.

Peppers
Filled Pastries

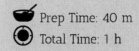

Prep Time: 40 m
Total Time: 1 h

Servings per Recipe: 10
Calories   342.0
Fat   3.6g
Cholesterol   0.0mg
Sodium   4.0mg
Carbohydrates   66.1g
Protein   10.2g

Ingredients

4 onions
2 tbsps concentrated tomato puree
2 green peppers
2 tbsps olive oil
salt & pepper
1 hot pepper
500 g fine semolina

250 g plain flour
salt
water

Directions

1. For filling, core the peppers and cut into fine strips and then cut the onions into rings.
2. In a skillet, heat a little oil and sauté the peppers and onions till softened.
3. Stir in the tomato puree, salt and black pepper and simmer, covered for about 5 minutes.
4. Remove from heat and let it cool.
5. For pastry, in a bowl mix the semolina, flour and salt.
6. With your hands, make a well in the center of the mixture.
7. Slowly, add the required amount of water and knead for about 8-10 minutes till a stiff dough forms.
8. Divide the dough and then roll into golf sized balls.
9. Place the balls, one at a time onto a greased surface and stretch out thinly.
10. Divide the filling mixture in the center of each pastry and fold all the edges, one at a time to form a square parcel.
11. In a large skillet, heat the oil and fry the parcels till golden brown from both sides.

NORTH AFRICAN
Vanilla Bread

Prep Time: 3 h
Total Time: 3 h 10 m

Servings per Recipe: 1
Calories	260.6
Fat	11.3g
Cholesterol	29.1mg
Sodium	20.0mg
Carbohydrates	34.0g
Protein	5.5g

Ingredients
1 kg all-purpose flour
1 C. ghee or 1 C. butter
1/2 C. cream
1 pinch salt
1/2 tsp vanilla
2 tbsp instant yeast
3 - 4 tbsp sugar
1/2 liter sour milk or 1/2 liter yogurt

1 tbsp anise
1 tbsp fennel seed
1 tbsp sesame seeds

Directions
1. Get a large mixing bowl: Combine in it the four with sugar, seeds, yeast, vanilla and salt. Mix them well.
2. Place a small saucepan over medium heat. Melt the butter in it. Transfer it to the flour mix. Mix them well.
3. Combine in the yogurt with cream. Mix them well with your hands until your get a smooth dough. Place a kitchen towel over the dough and let it rise for 30 min.
4. Divide the dough into several egg sized pieces. Cover them with a kitchen towel and let them rise for 2 h 10 min.
5. Place a piece of dough in a floured working surface. Roll it in the shape of circle with you hands. Repeat the process with the rest of the dough.
6. Place the dough circles on greased baking sheets and let them rest for 1 h.
7. Before you do anything preheat the oven to 356 F.
8. Get a small mixing bowl: Whisk in it some milk with vanilla and an egg. Make several parallel lines with a knife on top of the bread circles.
9. Brush them with the vanilla mix. Cook them in them for 16 min. Serve your bread warm with some sweet or savory toppings.
10. Enjoy.

Egyptian
Stuffed Grape Leaves

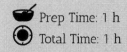 Prep Time: 1 h
◉ Total Time: 1 h

Servings per Recipe: 20
Calories   111.5
Fat   7.0g
Cholesterol   20.1mg
Sodium   135.8mg
Carbohydrates   6.0g
Protein   5.4g

Ingredients

1 1/4 lbs ground beef
3/4 C. long grain rice, cooked
1 small onion, chopped fine
2 garlic cloves, crushed or minced)
1 tsp salt
1/4 tsp black pepper
1/4 tsp ground cumin

1 (1 quart) jar pickled grape leaves, in brine, well rinsed and drained, stems cut off
2 tbsp olive oil
1 tbsp lemon juice

Directions

1. Get a large mixing bowl: Combine in it the beef with rice, onion, garlic, cumin, salt and pepper. Mix them well.
2. Shape some of mix into strip like your index finger. Place a grape leaf over a working surface. Place the stuffing log in the middle of the leaf.
3. Lay the bottom and upper sides over the filling and roll it. Place it in a greased casserole dish. Repeat the process with the rest of the ingredients.
4. Lay the stuffed leaves in a greased casserole pan without leaving any emptiness between them. Pour enough water to cover the stuffed leaves.
5. Drizzle the lemon juice with olive oil and stir them gently. Place it over high medium heat. Cook it until it starts boiling. Lower the heat and cook it for 22 min.
6. Serve your stuffed leaves warm.
7. Enjoy.

Fish Fillet
Salad

🍲 Prep Time: 15 m
⏱ Total Time: 30 m

Servings per Recipe: 4
Calories	226.8
Fat	9.1g
Cholesterol	143.5mg
Sodium	473.5mg
Carbohydrates	7.6g
Protein	28.4g

Ingredients

3/4 lb. lean white fish fillet, skin and bones removed
1/2 lb. medium shrimp, raw, shelled and deveined
1 tomatoes
1 bell pepper, peeled, seeded and cut into thin strips
1 tbsp fresh flat leaf parsley, chopped

2 small red hot peppers, seeded and chopped
2 garlic cloves, chopped
1/4 C. fresh lime juice (or lemon juice)
2 tbsp extra virgin olive oil
1 tbsp tomato paste
1/2 tsp salt

Directions

1. In a large skillet of the boiling water, poach the fish for about 5 minutes.
2. With a slotted spatula, transfer the fish into a bowl.
3. In the same simmering water, poach the shrimp for about 2-4 minutes.
4. With a slotted spatula, transfer the shrimp into the bowl of fish, reserving 2/3 C. of the poaching liquid.
5. Peel and seed the tomato and then, chop the tomato flesh.
6. In the bowl of the seafood, add the tomatoes, peppers, parsley and garlic and gently, toss to coat.
7. In a small pan, add the lemon juice, olive oil, tomato paste, salt and reserved poaching liquid and bring to a boil.
8. Reduce the heat and simmer, uncovered for about 5 minutes.
9. Pour the sauce over the salad mixture and gently, stir to cobine.
10. Keep aside at room temperature for at least 30 minutes before serving.

North African
Spiced Up Beans

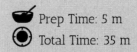 Prep Time: 5 m

Total Time: 35 m

Servings per Recipe: 4

Calories	139.4
Fat	0.7g
Cholesterol	0.0mg
Sodium	14.9mg
Carbohydrates	25.8g
Protein	8.9g

Ingredients
1 (15 oz) cans cooked fava beans or 1 1/2 C. cooked fava beans
1 small onion, chopped
3 garlic cloves, chopped
1 large tomatoes, chopped
1/2 tsp chili powder
1/2 tsp curry powder
1/2 tsp cumin
1 dash cinnamon
1 dash clove

1 dash turmeric
1 dash cayenne
1 tbsp lemon juice
salt
1 small potato, peeled and cooked, added when onion is cooking (optional)

Directions
1. Place a large pan over medium heat. Heat a splash of oil in it. Sauté in it the onion for 3 min. Stir in the garlic and cook them for 1 min.
2. Stir in the tomato and cook them for 4 min until it softens. Stir in the lemon juice with spices, a pinch of salt and pepper.
3. Cook them for 18 min over low heat while stirring them occasionally. Serve it with some extra olive oil.
4. Enjoy.

West
African Curry

Prep Time: 1 h 30 m
Total Time: 2 h

Servings per Recipe: 4
Calories   612.2
Fat   14.4g
Cholesterol   82.9mg
Sodium   363.8mg
Carbohydrates   86.5g
Protein   31.7g

Ingredients
1 lb lean stewing beef
1 small. onion
2 small bell peppers
1 (14 1/2 oz.) cans diced tomatoes
2 tbsp curry powder
1/2 tsp salt

2 C. rice
raisins

Directions
1. Cut the beef into 1/2-inch cubes.
2. Chop the onion and peppers.
3. In a large pan, add the beef, onions, peppers, undrained tomatoes, curry powder and salt and bring to a boil.
4. Reduce the heat and simmer for about 1 1/2-2 hours.
5. Meanwhile, prepare the rice according to package's directions.
6. Serve the beef over the rice with a topping of the some raisins.

Made in the
USA
Monee, IL